The Greatest Five

Glenn Sprich

Copyright © 2019
Glenn Sprich
Saint Louis, Missouri

All Rights Reserved

Library of Congress Control Number: 2019930393

ISBN 978-0-9600809-1-5

No part of this publication may by reproduce in any
form or by any means without prior written
permission from the author
except that brief portions may be quoted for a
review.

Correspondence and orders may be sent to:

Glenn Sprich
www.biblestudiesforthecommonman.com
studiesbibleglenn@gmail.com

DEDICATION

This book is dedicated to
the men and women who lived out
the events in this book. May their
love for God and their love for
His Church inspire us today.

CONTENTS

	ACKNOWLEDGMENTS	i
	FORWARD	1
1	PENTECOST	3
2	PHILIP CONVERTS THE ETHIOPIAN EUNUCH	19
3	THE CONVERSION OF SAUL	37
4	PETER CONVERTS CORNELIUS	53
5	THE COUNCIL OF JERUSALEM	67
6	FINAL THOUGHTS	89
	SOURCES	91
	ABOUT THE AUTHOR	92

ACKNOWLEDGMENTS

One of my wife's favorite sayings is "it takes a village to raise a child." It also "takes a village" to write a book. I would like to thank "the village" of people in my life who specifically impacted me in writing this book.

Thank you to: My wife, Patti, who first encouraged me to even write this book. I would never have been able to finish this book without her patience and computer help. Most important of all, she exemplifies God's love to everyone she meets, graciously living out the themes of faith in this book.

My writing coach, Janet Kraus, who guided me every step of the way, encouraging and advising me from the beginning of the writing process to the conclusion of publishing.

My editor, Pam Wallace, who took my thoughts, feelings, and words and put them together to form a readable, cohesive, and enjoyable book to read.

My daughter-in-law, Laura Sprich, for designing the front and back covers, drawing the maps for each chapter, and all of her additional technical support.

My friend, Joan Gooris, for proofing the rough drafts. Her feedback that she provided was invaluable in helping me with my content and information flow.

Liz Martinez, who advised me about the writing process and connected me with my editor.

Liz Kelly of No Waste Publishing for her guidance and professional publishing of this book.

Pastor Gary Schimmer, who guided me through the publishing process having written his own book.

To all of my pastors through the years - men called by God who taught and preached the Good News of salvation through Jesus Christ directly to me: Pastor Martin Heinche; Pastor Edwin Dubberke; Pastor Al Erdman; Pastor Michael Bronner; Pastor Martin Brauer; Pastor Rudolph Prange; Pastor Rich Wilson; Pastor Rob Kasper; Pastor Dan Teuscher; Pastor Bill Geis; Pastor Brian King; Pastor David Peter; Pastor Joel Biermann; and Pastor Joel Christiansen who as my Pastor exemplifies what a man of God is through his love of God, love of God's church and his love for the members of Webster Gardens Lutheran Church.

Finally, all of the people who attended small group and Sunday morning Bible classes with me. Just regular Christian men and women who love God, love each other, and show the love of Jesus to people they meet. During small groups and Sunday Bible class discussions, they shared their faith, their life experiences, and how they are helping the Christian Church grow today and, in the generations, to come.

FORWARD

Christians today have the benefit of over two thousand years of established church history. We have multiple translations of the Bible, as well as countless books and studies about Holy Scripture. We also have TV, radio, movies, and the latest social media options to help us grow in our relationship with Jesus Christ.

We often take all of these resources for granted because they have always been part of our Christian faith and worship. The Christians in the early church did not have the vast resources that we enjoy today. They started their faith walk with one belief - that Jesus of Nazareth was the Messiah and that He shed His blood for the forgiveness of sins and through His resurrection we can receive the gift of eternal life. As the early Church developed, it laid the foundation for the Church today.

This book was written to help us learn from the example of these early Christians. Written by a Christian layman for Christian laymen, this study is easy to read and understand. It will help you to empathize with the intense struggles Christians had starting the early Christian Church. This book will give you some insight into the experiences of the early Christian Church and five major events that shaped its development. Each chapter has seven parts: background to set the stage for the event; an expanded version of what happened during the event; an introduction to the major people involved in the event; the effect of the event on the early Church as well as the Church today; an analysis of "what if" the event hadn't happen; discussion questions; and three action steps to challenge you to live out the lessons learned from the event.

The early Christians certainly lived in interesting and challenging times just like we do today. The Holy Spirit is alive and thriving today just like in the early church, the Gospel is being proclaimed to people in every country in the world, the church is facing persecution around the globe and still growing in spite of that, Christians everywhere are daily living their faith in honor of Jesus, and we are strong in our practice and defense of our doctrines and beliefs especially in face of opposition of secular America.

Have a meaningful time reading this book and may God bless you on your study.

Glenn Sprich   December 2018

CHAPTER 1

PENTECOST
"THE HOLY SPIRIT EXPLODES"

ACTS 2

"THEY SAW WHAT SEEMED TO BE TONGUES OF FIRE THAT SEPARATED AND CAME TO REST ON EACH OF THEM. ALL OF THEM WERE FILLED WITH THE HOLY SPIRIT AND BEGAN TO SPEAK IN OTHER TONGUES AS THE SPIRIT ENABLED THEM."
ACTS 2:3-4

Pentecost is widely viewed as "The Birthday of the Church". It's a familiar story of the Disciples huddled together some fifty days after the resurrection of Jesus. The followers of Jesus which at one time numbered in the thousands had dwindled to less than two hundred and the remaining Disciples were left wondering how they were to accomplish the task Jesus had left them. They could not comprehend how their small group were to go into the world and make disciples of all nations. All nations? How were they to do that? Their leader, Jesus, was gone. Would they be next to be arrested and crucified?

Close to 60 to 70 percent of Jews in the world at that time did not live in Palestine. The Jewish nation had been scattered (due to war, persecution, and expulsion) in the Great Diaspora following the Assyrian (722 B.C.) and Babylonian (586 B.C.) captivities. During the five hundred years that followed these captivities Jews traveled to areas as far as Western Europe, Africa, and throughout the Middle East, settling mainly in large urban cities. This gave them an opportunity to blend in with the local population and assimilate into new cultures. Along with their native language, they learned Greek, which was spoken throughout the modern world as the language of commerce and culture.

Despite the attempts to completely assimilate into the cultures of their new homes, the Jewish people hung onto the traditions and customs of their faith and race. They continued to worship one God though they were surrounded by peoples who practiced the worship of many gods. Each Jewish community had a neighborhood synagogue (meaning "gathering of people") where they came together to celebrate the Sabbath and religious festivals, share meals, educate children, settle disputes, and practice their religious rites and observance of the law. During the Great Diaspora, Jewish scholars also translated the Old Testament from Hebrew into Greek so every educated Jew and postulate could read and discuss the Scriptures no matter where they lived or language they spoke.

Much of the known world at that time had been conquered by and was ruled by Rome. Besides having an unstoppable army, the Romans were a people of builders. Not only did the Romans build magnificent structures and cities, they also built lots of roads. Roman leaders knew the value of commerce and the ability to quickly move armies around their empire. This road system enabled them to do that plus it made it convenient for Jews to make pilgrimages to Jerusalem for festival observances.

Our stage is set as Jewish pilgrims, numbering in the thousands, arrived in Jerusalem from places like Pamphylia,

Cappadocia, Mesopotamia, and Rome, to celebrate the annual observance of the Feast of Weeks, also known as the Festival of the Harvest. This was a seven-week period beginning on the first day of Passover through the fall harvest. In Greek, it was known as Pentecost, meaning 50 days. It was a joyful time thanking God for His blessing of the harvest and was outlined in Exodus 23: "Celebrate the Festival of Harvest with the first fruits of the crops you sow in your field.

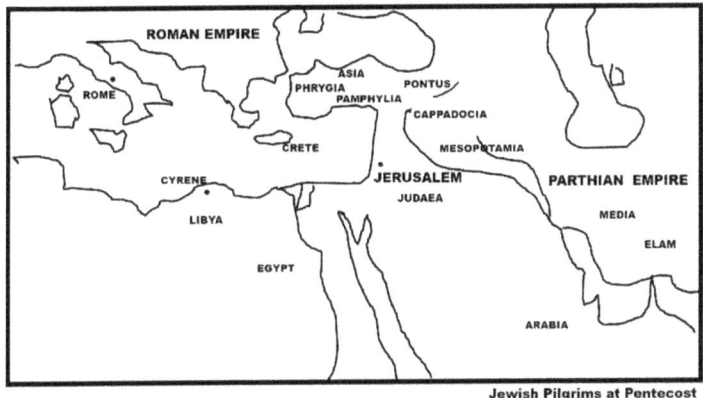

Jewish Pilgrims at Pentecost

THE EVENT

On the day of Pentecost, the twelve Disciples were gathered together in secluded room in Jerusalem when suddenly a sound like a violent wind tore through the house where they were! It appeared like "tongues of fire" on the heads of each of the Disciples (the presence of God has always been associated with wind and fire). Frightened, yet excited, they could feel the Holy Spirit enter into each of their hearts. Amazed, they thought to themselves: "We've never felt this excitement, this joy before. We can't believe what is happening. Jesus promised to send the Holy Spirit, but we never imagined this!" Perhaps the words of John the Baptist came to mind: "I baptize you with water but one who is more powerful than I will come, the straps of whose sandals I am not worthy to untie. He will baptize you with the Holy Spirit and fire." Or perhaps the words of Jesus' promise "the Father will give you an Advocate to help you and be with you forever, the Spirit of truth. But the Advocate, the Holy Spirit, whom the Father will send in my name, will teach you all things and will remind you of everything I have said to you." At the ascension of Jesus, He commissioned the Disciples "in the name of the Father, in the name of the Son and in the name of the Holy Spirit." The Disciples were so excited they burst into the street, shouting in all different languages, "What's going on? What's happening here? How is this possible that I'm talking in a foreign language I've never spoken before?"

The sound of the violent wind had drawn a crowd and the Disciples began to exclaim in amazement to those around them. Although people from many nations who spoke different languages were among the crowd that gathered around the Disciples, the Disciples realized that everyone could understand what was being said! Each of the Disciples was speaking in a foreign language! "This isn't Aramaic? How can I speak like this? It is the Holy Spirit. It must be a God thing!"

This ability to speak in other languages is referred to in Greek as Xenolalia - "many languages." Remember the Sunday school story of the Tower of Babel in Genesis 11?

"Now the whole world was one language...let us build a tower that reaches into the heavens...if as one people speaking the same language...they think that nothing they do will be impossible...I will confuse their language and scatter them."

God created different languages because men were using their unity for evil purposes. Now, thanks to the redemptive work of Jesus on the cross, God sent the Holy Spirit to bridge the barrier different languages had created.

The crowd was amazed that the Disciples were speaking in different languages. They said to one another, "aren't these men Galileans? Don't they all speak Aramaic? How is it that I can understand them?" All stood in wonder at what was happening, but some just assumed that the uproar was caused by the Disciples having been out drinking already.

Yes, these Disciples were just ordinary men from Galilee. Before Jesus called them, they were ordinary men with families, jobs, and regular lives. Why these men? Maybe because of their faith (or lack of faith), their unique personalities, or their situation in life. They probably had a normal Jewish upbringing and were familiar with the Old Testament scriptures containing all the stories, laws, customs, and rituals of their faith. But many of them were "unschooled, ordinary men." Despite this, or possibly because of it, Jesus handpicked each of them. After three years walking alongside Jesus, learning His teachings, seeing him perform miracles, heal the sick, give sight to the blind, even raise the dead - these men were changed. Others around them "took note that these men had been with Jesus." But even after sitting at Jesus' feet and listening to His teachings and parables, the Disciples still did not quite understand. Thus, enters the Holy Spirit.

Peter could not contain himself - he was so excited! He ran to the temple with the other Disciples where Jews were worshiping. Peter and the Disciples climbed to the top steps of the temple, and turning, Peter addressed the crowd:"

"Fellow Jews of Jerusalem and all who are visiting here today, listen to me. The twelve of us haven't been drinking, it's only 9:00 in the morning - not enough time to get drunk even if we had started drinking when we got up this morning. Hear me out. The prophet Joel said that God would give His Spirit to all people to experience His wondrous love and salvation. When the end of the world comes, if your heart belongs to God in the right way, you will be saved. Previously God's Spirit was only accessible to a chosen few but now, God's Spirit is on every-one, both men and women. His Spirit will enable us to experience things we never dreamed of and our belief in Jesus will save us. Jesus of Nazareth, who having the power of God, did miraculous healings and teachings. According to God's plan, Jesus was crucified by the Romans and died. But that wasn't the end! God brought Jesus back to life as part of His plan for our salvation. Even David tells us in Psalm 16 that one day one of His descendants would not stay in the grave but be raised. It gave David and all of us the hope that one day one of David's descendants would be the Messiah. We no longer have to wait in hope for that day to come. It has come! Jesus of Nazareth is the Messiah that David was pointing to. God raised Jesus from the dead back to life. I, Peter, saw this. We, His disciples saw the resurrected Jesus! Jesus is now sitting at the right of God, and has sent us the Holy Spirit. That is what you are here experiencing today! I can't say it any clearer, Jesus of Nazareth, God's Son, is the Messiah!"

As Peter spoke, the other Disciples translated his words into all the languages of those present. Upon hearing the message, the people asked themselves:

"How do I respond to this? What just came over me? Why am I feeling both sad, hurt in my heart that my sins could have done this to cause the death of Jesus and also happy that God accomplished His plan of cleansing my sins and giving me salvation? Could this really be true? After all those years of waiting for the Messiah, could now be the time? Jesus of Nazareth, the Messiah? YES! Jesus of Nazareth is the promised Messiah! But now where do I go from here? How do I respond? What shall I do?"

Peter replied:

"Repent and be baptized, every one of you, in the name of Jesus Christ for the forgiveness of your sins and you will receive the gift of the Holy Spirit just as we have today. The promise is for you and your children and for all who are far off. It is for all whom the Lord our God will call."

About 3000 people came forward that morning to publicly express their changed lives and to be baptized. Wow! Talk about an altar call! Peter and the Disciples continued to share their faith in Jesus throughout the day with the men and women wanting to change to a new way of thinking, a new way of living, a new relationship with God the Father through Jesus Christ.

THE PEOPLE

At the time of Pentecost, the Disciples were all about twenty to thirty years old and all Galileans except Judas. Peter and his brother Andrew were fishermen from Bethsaida along with James and John who were nick named "Sons of Thunder". Fishing was a tough business with long hours in a boat in the hot sun or cold of night, wrestling with nets hopefully hauling in lots of fish. Maybe these four were just a bunch of loud and rough men who were well-matched to their rough and difficult profession. Yet, Jesus called each of them to be His Disciples. Andrew was originally a disciple of John the Baptist and told Peter that he had found the Messiah after meeting Jesus. Peter, James, and John were in the inner circle of Jesus' disciples and had the privilege of witnessing the Transfiguration, the raising of Jarius' daughter, and other events. John was known as "the disciple whom Jesus loved" and he wrote about his first-hand experience of the life of Jesus in his Gospel along with writing the letters of First, Second, and Third John and Revelation. His brother James later was the only one of the twelve Disciples mentioned in Acts to be martyred - killed by the sword.

Philip also was from Bethsaida. His occupation isn't mentioned but it seems that he was a close friend of another disciple, Nathanael. After meeting Jesus Philip exclaimed to Nathanael "We have found the one Moses and the prophets were talking about!" Philip was a problem solver, always trying to help, especially with the feeding of the 5000 and his request at the Last supper asking Jesus, "Lord, show us the Father." His friend Nathanael (Bar-Tolmi) came from Cana. He asked of Jesus "can anything good come out of Nazareth?" Despite Nathanael's doubt about whether Jesus was the Messiah, Jesus identified him as "a true Israelite in whom there is nothing false." Later, Nathanael was martyred for his faith in Jesus.

Matthew or Levi, the son of Alphaeus, came from Capernaum and was a despised tax collector who was considered a traitor by the Jewish people and a puppet of the Roman authorities. He made his money by overcharging on taxes and getting Jews to pay more than "what is due Caesar." Yet, Jesus called Matthew who later recorded his wonderful eyewitness account of the ministry of Jesus in his Gospel. Next is James the Less whose parents would also become followers of Jesus.

Thaddaeus, Judas Son of James, was given the name "Labbacus" meaning "breast child," which we would today call a mama's boy. Maybe he was just a kind, compassionate guy who loved his mom. In John 14 at the last supper he asked Jesus "why do you intend to show yourself to us Lord, and not the world?" Thomas, Didymus (meaning twin), was a fisherman like some of the other disciples. His doubting made him famous or infamous depending on your point of view. He only believed that Jesus rose from the dead when he actually saw Jesus and put his hand into the side of Jesus where the Roman spear had pierced Him. In Church tradition, Thomas was killed by a spear - a spear that pierced his own side just like his Savior, Jesus.

Simon the Zealot, was named because of his strong enthusiasm and patriotism or perhaps he could have been a passionate Jewish nationalist, a terrorist opposed to foreign occupation of Israel, or a combination of both. The newest disciple, Matthias, was chosen to replace Judas to round out the Twelve at the time of the Pentecost.

A group of ordinary guys, with ordinary lives that after walking with Jesus and receiving the Holy Spirit at Pentecost were changed forever into extra ordinary men with extra ordinary accomplishments. The indwelling of the Holy Spirit in the Disciples reminded them that Jesus had left them a job to do. And they finally felt equipped to do the job. They were ready to go out into the world and spread the Good News of Jesus. They no longer were paralyzed by fear. Jesus and the Holy Spirit were with them and "If they are with me, who can be against me." The Disciples, through the Holy Spirit, were given Spiritual Gifts: administration, hospitality, encouragement, discernment, knowledge, leadership, healing, prophesy, serving, shepherding, teaching, wisdom, and evangelism. They also had the Fruits of the Spirit: love, joy, peace, patience, kindness, goodness, faithfulness, gentleness and self-control. These Disciples, this "band of brothers", were ready to take on the world for Jesus!

THE EFFECT

What was the effect of the first Pentecost on the people that were present in Jerusalem that day? What was the effect of the Pentecost on the growth of the early Church? First, it expanded by 3000 new members in one day! That's a lot of people. In one day, the Church expanded about fifteen times its size. Those that were baptized were radically changed and left with questions on how to mesh their Jewish beliefs and practices with their new faith in Jesus as the Messiah. They also went back to the nations where they had come from and spread the Good News of Jesus and what they had experienced of the Holy Spirit. Within fifty days of the death and resurrection of

Jesus, His story was spreading to over sixteen countries in over sixteen languages. As these new Christians went home, they started new "Churches" in their home towns, providing places to learn, share, grow, and fellowship together.

The growth of the early Church and the questions about how to live out their new faith, led to the need to address various issues such as creating a model of how to organize worship services and care for those in need. The early Christians met together in their homes, shared the teachings of the apostles, and ate meals together. Though they came from different backgrounds, those in the early Church were united by their belief in Jesus and they worked together to set up ways to ensure that everyone in their community was cared for both spiritually and physically. Their unity, strong faith, and love put into actions in their community, was rewarded with their numbers continuing to increase as their family, friends, and neighbors came to faith in Jesus. However, with this growth, came much persecution for these new Christians. Despite this persecution, the early Church continued to grow.

Later Paul, Peter, and the other Apostles went on missionary journeys throughout the countries in and around Palestine. Many people were eager to learn more about Jesus and these missionary journeys aided in the expansion of the early Church and bringing order to some of the confusion caused when people from various religious and cultural backgrounds came together through their faith in Jesus. The Apostles established mission efforts and doctrines that are still used by Christians today.

Finally, Pentecost established Peter as the head of the early Church. Jesus commissioned Peter as the head of His Church and on that first Pentecost, through the Holy Spirit, Peter stepped up as the leader of the Church. Catholics the world over believe that Jesus installed Peter as the first Pope, the head of the Catholic Church, passing on "The Shoes of the

Fisherman" to each new Pope.

What effect does the first Pentecost have on us today? The Christian Church today has over 2.4 billion members. It has grown from a small Jewish sect into the largest religion in the world practiced by people in every continent. The entire Bible (Old and New Testaments together) have been translated into over 600 languages and dialects and the New Testament into over 1500 languages and dialects, making the Bible available in almost every known language in the world and ensuring that people everywhere have an opportunity to study God's Word for themselves. As Peter gave his sermon on the steps of the temple of Jerusalem on that first Pentecost, who could have imagined the that the Good News of Jesus would someday be shared over the radio, television, and social media? Pretty soon every person in the world will have a smart phone or some other communication devise and it is our prayer that technology will continue to be used to share God's Word. God still pours out His Holy Spirit to us today. He calls, gathers, and enlightens members of His Church every day. He challenges us to use our spiritual gifts and the fruits of the Spirit each day. As a Church, we try to emulate the early Church as it was laid out in Acts, fellowshipping, praying, worshiping, studying the Bible, partaking of the Sacraments, and serving together in the bond of unity. People throughout the World today are coming to Jesus the same way as they did on that first Pentecost through hearing the Word of God preached, opening their heart and mind to Jesus, repenting of their sins, and acknowledging Jesus as their Lord and Savior. For over 2000 years the Church has been growing and will continue to grow until the return of Jesus.

Is the Church today experiencing a similar growth explosion like on Pentecost and in the immediate days/years that followed? It seems that the Church is actually declining in numbers in the West, mainly North America and Western Europe. For centuries these areas have had phenomenal growth and expansion of the Church through the advent of technology and missionary efforts. However, with population declining and the emphasis on self-reliance and material wealth, the principles of Christianity have slowly been omitted from the lives of Americans and those in Western Europe. But the reverse is happening in other areas of the world. Christianity is seeing an unprecedented growth expansion in African, the Arabian Peninsula, and Eastern Asia. Soon these areas will have more Christians than the western areas of the world. The challenge is how to get the abundant resources in the West to the areas of the world that are growing the fastest. We just need to trust the Holy Spirit to direct us how to use our resources in the best ways.

THE WHAT IF

What if Pentecost never happened? What would have happened to the Disciples and how would the growth of the early Church been effected? We can only imagine and speculate about the consequences of the first Pentecost not happening. We can be sure that one way or another, God's plan of salvation for all people would have been realized. But, let's consider what might have happened.

First, the Disciples were huddled together, without a leader, confused, scared, and with no game plan on what they were going to do next. Sure, they had been given the Great Commission, but how were they to carry it out? Without the gift of the Holy Spirit, the Disciples would probably have gone back to their regular homes and jobs just like they did right after the resurrection of Jesus. They would have gone fishing!

Secondly, many of the actions of Peter up until Pentecost did not inspire confidence in him as a leader. However, there was no one else ready and willing to step up to the plate and be the new leader of the Church, especially since they were probably still "wanted" men.

The fear that, having eliminated Jesus, the Pharisees and teachers of the law would try to go after His remaining Disciples to crush the Jesus movement forever. In eliminating the twelve Disciples, the several hundred remaining followers of Jesus would not have had any leadership and clear, accurate theology of this new faith to follow.

Additionally, without the baptism of the Holy Spirit occurring, Pentecost would have been just another annual pilgrimage for the Jews that had gathered from all around the world. No Holy Spirit, no baptism, no changed lives. The Jews would have returned to their home to continue in their old way of faith, being good Jews and following the Torah. Although the Gospel would surely have spread, there would have been no explosion in the numbers that were coming to faith in Jesus Christ. Without the rapid spread of the Gospel to other areas of the world, the early Church would have been in grave danger of extinction when 35 years later (70AD) the Romans destroyed the Temple in Jerusalem.

THE DISCUSSION

1.) If you, as a lifelong Jew, were present at that first Pentecost in Jerusalem, how would you have responded to Peter's words? What effect would hearing his message in your own language have had on you? Would you have believed that Jesus of Nazareth was the Messiah? Why? How would it have changed your life?

2.) What can we, as individuals, a local congregation, a denomination, the Christian Church, do to spread the saving Gospel of Jesus Christ to people of every language and culture in our community, in our country, and in our world today?

3.) How does the Holy Spirit work in your life today? How does the Holy Spirit work in the Christian Church today?

4.) Other than Peter, James, and John, there is no further mention of the nine other Disciples in rest of Scripture. What do you think they did after Pentecost? Why did the Disciples (Peter was involved in two other events) only have a vital role in one event that we are studying, Pentecost?

5.) How does your local congregation emulate the example of the early Church in Acts 2:42-47?

THE ACTION

1.) This week, find at least one additional way to be involved with your local congregation, your denomination, or the Christian Church at large using your own personal resources of time, talent, and treasure.

2.) Be in the Word everyday letting the Holy Spirit increase your faith and grow in your relationship with Jesus Christ as your Lord and Savior.

3.) Be excited about sharing God's love and the gift of salvation in Jesus with everyone you meet.

THE PRAYER

Dear Heavenly Father,
Thank you for the gift of Your Holy Spirit so I too can confess and accept Jesus into my life as Lord and Savior. Please increase that Spirit in me as I praise and worship You. Guide me to serve Your Church with my time, my talents, and my treasures. Thank you for the Disciples who went before us at that first Pentecost and established the early Church in the face of so much persecution, eventually giving their lives so that the Good News of Jesus would spread though out the world. May we, as disciples of Jesus, continue to live, to teach, to preach the love of Jesus to everyone everywhere. Amen.

CHAPTER 2

PHILIP CONVERTS THE ETHIOPIAN EUNUCH "THE COLOR OF THE CHURCH"

ACTS 8

"THE EUNUCH ASKED PHILIP 'TELL ME PLEASE, WHO IS THE PROPHET TALKING ABOUT, HIMSELF OR SOMEONE ELSE?'"
ACTS 8:34

The word of today is diversity. Diversity in our neighborhoods, diversity in our schools, diversity in our politics, diversity in our churches. We are a nation of diversity. People came to America mainly from all parts of Western and Eastern Europe, Asia and Africa seeking a better life, a fresh start, and a life free of poverty, persecution, and class or social discrimination. It was a difficult beginning for our country, as we attempted to blend together so many languages, customs, and religious practices. But through the years we made it work. We went from a mélange of people, to becoming the United States of America, blending our diverse traditions and cultural backgrounds to form a new identity - Americans.

Today, people are immigrating to America primarily from Asia, Central & South America, Africa, and the Middle East. They come to America with the same dreams and seeking the same opportunities that millions of immigrants to America before sought. Those of us already established as Americans struggle with this influx of diverse immigrants. People that look, talk, and act differently than we do. Do we let them into our country, into our way of life? Will they fit in?

The Church today also struggles with diversity. It is said that the greatest time of segregation in our country is the hour we spend in Church each Sunday. How many congregations do you know of that have a mixture of different races, cultures, social and economic groups? Christianity is often seen by people around the world as a religion of white, Western Europeans. The question for the Church today is, how do we embrace the diversity all around us? How do we, as Christians, respond to this current wave of immigrants? Can we bring them the Good News of salvation through Jesus Christ?

While Christianity is declining in the "West" today, it is experiencing explosive growth in Africa and Asia. The message of salvation is for all people but how should we reach out to people of other races, cultures, languages both here in America and abroad? In the New Testament, we read about Philip stepping out of his cultural comfort zone and taking on a mission that maybe only a few others would have dared to try. He looked beyond the race, culture, social traits of people, to see fellow brothers and sisters in need of Jesus Christ.

Philip, one of "The Seven" in Acts 6, was commissioned in Jerusalem as the church was undergoing tremendous growth and began to face intense persecution because of its growth. This persecution resulted in the arrest and stoning of Stephen, also one of "The Seven." The situation in Jerusalem became so dangerous for Christians that many of them left and scattered throughout the Galilean and Judean countryside. Due to the persecution of the church, Philip chose to go north to minister to the people of Samaria. Although it was a somewhat difficult and challenging task, through the gift of the Holy Spirit he began teaching and preaching. He also performed miracles such as healing the sick and driving out impure spirits. His ministry to the Samaritan people was quickly rewarded as they began to believe that Jesus Christ was their Lord and Savior.

Philip's ministry to the Samaritan people was not something a pious Jew would do. The Jews looked down on the Samaritan people as "half breeds," not worth their time or effort. Later in his ministry he even encountered a black man. How many people from Africa came to Jerusalem? Probably not many! So when Philip encountered the Eunuch from Ethiopia, he not only had to overcome his prejudice of seeing a man of a different color but also a rich, powerful man from a different social and economic class. It took a lot of "guts" for Philip to take the initiative to approach him, but Philip did it. The Holy Spirit was with him and together they achieved miraculous results.

THE EVENT

One morning, as Philip was waking up, he was startled by a strange appearance in his room that looked like a person, yet was not a person. Philip immediately sensed that there was something different about this person and when this person spoke Philip knew it was no ordinary person but a messenger from God. This angel of the Lord said to Philip, "Go south to the road - the desert road that goes down from Jerusalem to Gaza." That was it! Short and sweet, yet completely clear instructions for Philip to follow. After delivering the command, the angel of the Lord disappeared! Philip could feel the strength of the Holy Spirit and the excitement of having a new mission. He immediately packed his bag, grabbed his staff and he journeyed south. He really didn't know what was going to happen to him but trusted in the Lord to guide him in what to do.

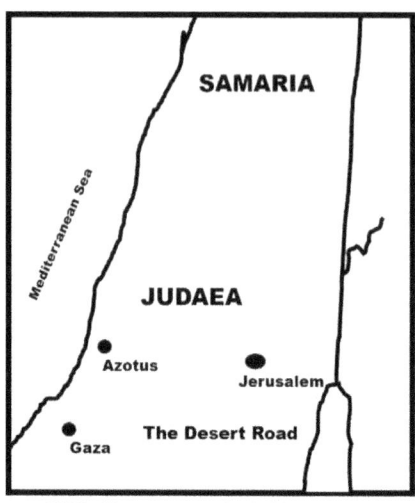

Philip Encounters the Ethiopian Eunuch

The desert road was about fifty miles away from where he was staying so it was going to take Philip two to three days just to reach the desert road before he would find out what God had planned for him. As Philip was walking south along the desert road, he came to a "rest stop." Not a rest stop like we find on a trip today where we stop for gas and lunch, but a stop perhaps under a shade tree for a brief respite from the hot sun and to get a cool drink of water from an oasis well. As he was resting under the tree, Philip spotted a strange group of men a short distance away. They too had stopped for rest and water but they were men who appeared to be of great importance and had skin as black as night. Philip had heard of people from other parts of the world that did not look like him and now he has seen some. These were men that you just didn't see every day in Judea!

One man in particular stood out. He was sitting in a chariot (Philip wished he could travel like that. It sure would beat walking!) reading a scroll. The man was dressed in fine white clothing with jewels on his fingers and a very tall, decorated turban, certainly a man of great wealth. He was accompanied by what looked like a driver, a personal secretary, servants and an armed escort. Suddenly, the Holy Spirit told Philip: "Walk to that chariot and see what they are doing." So that's just what Philip did! He got up, walked over to the chariot where the distinguished gentleman was sitting, and heard the man reading out loud in Greek from the book of Isaiah! Philip knew those words of Isaiah - had read them so many times that he practically had them memorized. How strange that this man who was obviously not an Israelite, was reading from Isaiah. Philip said to the man (In Greek because this man probably did not speak Hebrew or Aramaic): "Do you understand what you are reading?" The man looked up and replied, "How can I unless someone can explain it to me?"

The black man was amazed that this ordinary, Jewish looking man, was speaking to him in Greek. Greek was the language of commerce and culture of which Philip did not appear to have either. The black man introduced himself to Philip: "I am the Treasurer of Kandake, Queen of the Ethiopian people. I am on my way home after my pilgrimage to Jerusalem." Philip realized that, along with possessing wealth and position, this man must be a Eunuch due to his role in the royal court of the queen. Philip respectfully bowed and introduced himself.

The Eunuch addressed Philip:

"Here Philip, sit with me a short time while we rest and, as a Jew, please explain to me what Isaiah is talking about Here in chapter 53 verses –seven and eight - "He was lead like a sheep to the slaughter, and as a lamb before his shearer is silent, so he did not open his mouth. In his humiliation he was deprived of justice. Who can speak of his descendants? For his life was taken from this earth." Tell me Philip, who is the prophet talking about here, is he talking about himself or someone else?"

Philip responded:

"Isaiah isn't talking about himself. He's talking about the promised deliver, the Son of God, the Messiah that at that time was still to come. The Good News is that this deliverer is Jesus of Nazareth. Throughout scripture (the Old Testament) the prophets outlined the coming of the Messiah especially what you've been reading about in Isaiah. Earlier in Isaiah (chapter 7), he tells us about Jesus when he wrote that the virgin would conceive, give birth to a son, and call him Immanuel - 'God with us.' Later, Isaiah said (chapters 9 and 19) 'for unto us a child is born, a son is given to us. He will be called wonderful councilor, almighty God, everlasting Father, the Prince of Peace and His kingdom will have no end. He will sit on the throne of David and rule forever with truth and justice.' "

"The virgin that Isaiah is talking about is named Mary. I have met her. She's very active in The Way. I've talked with her many times about her Son, Jesus, and learned firsthand about His life and ministry. She was with Jesus from His birth until His ascension into heaven. She gave birth to Jesus in a stable in Bethlehem, just as the prophet Micah (chapter 4) told us! As Jesus grew up, the wisdom of the Lord and the Holy Spirit were in Him. His ministry brought hope, healing, and comfort, and He proclaimed that he had come to release us from the prison of sin and death (Isaiah 16). He set us on a new path and gave us a new way to have a relationship with God, our Father. A relationship of love, prayer, and service to Him and all men."

"But Jesus was rejected by His own people (Isaiah 53). He was betrayed by His friend and unjustly arrested, yet He remained silent before His accusers while He was beaten and humiliated. He was crucified as a common criminal, pouring out His blood for our transgressions. He took our sin, and the punishment we deserved, on Himself and was voluntarily led like a lamb to the slaughter, obeying God's will completely. His suffering paid the price of our sin - all sin - so we could have peace with God."

"The best news of all is that Jesus didn't stay in the grave! God raised Him up from the dead after three days, once and for all claiming victory over sin and death. All who believe in Him will be saved with that same power and have victory over sin and death. Now Jesus reigns in Heaven and sent the Holy Spirit to everyone who has faith in Jesus. And people of every nation, whether a Jew like me or a Gentile like you, will rest in His arms of salvation."

The Eunuch replied:

"Now that we have rested a while, we need to continue on our journey home. Philip will you please come with us for a little while so we can we talk some more about this Jesus, who is the Messiah?"

As they were traveling down the road, the Eunuch spotted another oasis in the distance which appeared to have a pool of water. He ordered his men to check and he was right, there was a pool of water that had not been evaporated by the sun. Stopping, the Eunuch excitedly jumped down from his chariot and wading into the pool of water turning around, he said:

"I know of the Jewish custom of baptism, which signifies a new life of repentance and change. I saw it once when I was in Jerusalem worshiping. It was done by a man named John who spoke of Jesus just like you. I didn't understand who Jesus was back then, but thanks to you, I know Him now. Philip, please baptize me. I want this new life in Jesus."

Philip walked into the pool, scooped up a handful of water, and poured it over the head of the bowing Eunuch three times.

"I baptize you in the name of the Father and of the Son and

of the Holy Spirit."

As the Eunuch looked up at Philip, a strange, new feeling of excitement came over him - a sense of joy and peace. He had never experienced anything like this before! He was amazed that even he, an outcast, a Eunuch, could be a follower of Jesus and receive the Holy Spirit. That the love of Jesus was in him!

The Eunuch embraced Philip and said, "Thank you Philip! Thank you for this great gift. I praise God for you and for Jesus, my Lord and Savior." As the Eunuch looked up into heaven to give thanks to God...Philip was gone! Vanished! Where did Philip go? The Eunuch shouted, "Praise God! Praise Jesus! Praise the Holy Spirit!" He could hardly wait to get back home and share this Good News about Jesus with everyone he knew.

As for Philip, one minute he was standing in a pool of water hugging the exuberant Eunuch and the next he was in Azotus, twenty miles away! Wow! How did that happen! Once again God showed Philip His many works and wonders. Philip realized that he was not far from his home town, so he decided to travel up the coast through Judea and Samaria until he reached his home in Caesarea. He was excited to continue preaching and teaching to parts of Samaria that he hadn't visited.

THE PEOPLE

There are a lot of Philips in the Bible. There is Philip, one of the twelve Disciples of Jesus and Philip the brother of Herod Antipas mentioned in Matthew 14. The Philip in our story is described in Acts 6 as one of "The Seven" and later in Acts as Philip the evangelist.

The Church was expanding so rapidly that additional

leaders were needed, especially leaders who had administrative and organizational skills along with a strong faith and the ability to teach and preach. Philip was chosen by the Disciples as one of "The Seven." Philip was chosen to be fair, kind, caring and to use the Church's resources wisely. He used his gifts to help resolve a dispute between Hebraic widows (Jewish women born, and living, in Judea) and Hellenistic widows (Jewish women living outside of Palestine). In addition to helping the Jewish widows, Philip took the Gospel to the Samaritans - Jews left behind in Israel that intermarried with non-Jews while the rest of the Jews went into captivity. When the exiled Jews came back home 70 years later, there was conflict because they wanted their land and homes back while the Samaritans felt they deserved to stay. A restless peace and segregation of the two people groups began. Most of all, Philip also stepped outside of his comfort zone to present the Gospel to a "man of color."

The Ethiopian Eunuch was only mentioned in Acts by where he was from and his title. A eunuch was a man that had been castrated, sometimes against their will. Castration was usually performed fairly young and to slaves or other men who wanted to serve the ruling royal family. The result of castration was an outward change of appearance due to hormone changes. These men often had higher pitch voices and did not grow beards or have any hair on their bodies. Since eunuchs were unable to have children, they were not a threat to the royals because they had no interest in overthrowing the current ruler so their children could inherit the kingdom. They had daily contact with the king and his family and often formed close, personal relationship with them. Being a eunuch, a Gentile, and "not whole" (not circumcised), he could only worship in the Court of the Gentiles in the temple in Jerusalem which was reserved for God fearers. (There are numerous references to Ethiopia in the Old Testament. Sometimes referred to as Nubia or Cush, there was certainly contact with Jews in Egypt and later through King Solomon and the Queen of Sheeba). As a God fearer, the Eunuch would have adopted some of the traditions and customs of the Jewish faith such as observing the major festivals and making regular pilgrimages to Jerusalem. After his baptism, he surely recalled the words of Isaiah 56: "to the eunuchs that keep my Sabbaths…I will give them an everlasting name…and who hold fast to my covenant…their burnt offerings and sacrifices will be accepted on my altar".

How different Philip and the Eunuch were: Philip was a Jew - the Eunuch was a Gentile; Philip was poor - the Eunuch was rich; Philip was of light colored skin - the Eunuch was black skinned; Philip had little education - the Eunuch had an extensive education; Philip knew Scripture well - the Eunuch did not. Yet, despite their differences, Philip presented the Gospel without hesitation to the Eunuch. Philip set the example for others to follow as one of the first missionaries to reach outside of Jewish Galilee and the Judean area. He set the example of expanding the church through diversity of culture, customs, language, and race. He believed that the saving gift of salvation through Jesus was for all people.

THE EFFECT

So, what effect did the conversion of the Eunuch have on Philip? Once again Philip experienced the hand of God in his ministry. God's direct command to go to the desert road, Philip meeting the Ethiopian Eunuch, the eunuch's subsequent acceptance of faith and baptism, and Philip's instant appearance miles away in Azotus - all of these were the work and blessing of the Holy Spirit in Philip's life. It certainly gave him confidence and strength to see such specific and dramatic results of his work. This confidence led him to live his life as a disciple of Jesus, commissioned to take the Good News to the ends of the earth. His life of faith also had a profound effect on his daughters and their belief in Jesus. Philip's experience with the Eunuch along with opportunities such as meeting with, and learning from, other great leaders of the early church (Peter, John, Paul, and Luke in Acts 21) greatly enhanced Philip's faith. Also, the effectiveness of Phillip's ministry undoubtedly validated his commission as one of "The Seven" and showed that the Holy Spirit would continue to bless the growth of the Church.

The Ethiopian Eunuch was also forever changed. The Eunuch could return home with confidence, joy, and excitement to share the Good News of Jesus with his family, friends, and those at his job. He had learned that there was no prejudice or exclusion with Jesus. It doesn't seem a stretch to imagine that the Eunuch made his home a place of discussion and learning where all people could grow in their faith in Jesus.

The conversion of the Ethiopian Eunuch had an immediate effect on the early church. First, it reinforced the knowledge that the saving Gospel of Jesus was for every tribe, nation, and people. Philip showed that there was great opportunity to spread the Gospel all over the world and should be shared with everyone. It didn't matter if the person was a Jew, Gentile, Greek, or African, the Good News was for everyone. Jesus commissioned the disciples to go and make disciples of all nations, to expand God's church and with Philip's conversion of the Eunuch, it expanded to a new continent - Africa! Also, by expanding the Church to a new country and continent, it may have expanded safely beyond any Jewish persecution and the Church could then grow, unhindered without Jewish interference.

Philip was an example of his calling to be able, ready, and willing to go where God called him to serve the church. He immediately left his surroundings and went where God directed him. What an example to other leaders in the early Church on how to carry out the Great Commission. The Apostles were very concerned about what would happen to the growth of the early Church after they were gone. How could they convey the joy, excitement, and value of their firsthand experience with Jesus to new church leaders who had not witnessed the personal ministry of Jesus?

Out of this concern, they chose "The Seven" and other leaders to continue the spread of the Gospel. The model the Apostles used to choose the next generation of church leaders became a standard that is still used in the Church today. They prayed for guidance from the Holy Spirit to choose men (and today women) who showed an exceptional love of God and the knowledge of God through prayer, studying the Scriptures, and teaching ability. The character of those chosen as leaders needed to be beyond approach and they were to be good husbands and fathers, leaders in their home, show integrity, have a good reputation, honest, hardworking, caring, and someone who loved his church members and the people in his community. Over the years, God's Church has grown because of the millions of men and women who have been chosen using this method as leaders in both the local and national churches to advance the Gospel of Jesus Christ.

The effect of the conversion of the Ethiopian Eunuch was phenomenal. What started out as a one-man mission to the people of Ethiopia, has now developed into a country of almost 45 million Christians. According to Church tradition, the Apostles Matthew or Bartholomew may have ventured as far south as the region of Ethiopia to minister to established Jewish/Christian communities. Today, Ethiopia is the only predominately Christian country in Africa. With 102 million people, Ethiopia is the second most populous country in Africa with approximately 43% of the people Christian and 33% Muslim. The largest national denomination is the Ethiopian Orthodox Christian Church.

While mainline Christianity is declining in "the West" due to materialism, secularism, and rationalism, these don't seem to be hindering factors in the African Christian Church today.

More and more people are moving away from the traditional African spiritual practices of their ancestors and responding to the Gospel, especially the Pentecostal expressions of faith. Africa is projected to grow in population in the next thirty years to 2 billion people out of a worldwide population of almost 9 billion people. Six of the twenty most populous nations of the world will be in Africa: Ethiopia, Congo, Uganda, Sudan, Nigeria, and Tanzania. Along with the growth of population, comes an opportunity for the Christian church to grow and to have a vital impact on people not only in Africa but also around the world. There are close to 380 million Christians in Africa today with a projected increase to 600 million by 2025! It is thought that by about 2050, Africa will be 40% Christian and 45% Muslim. An almost unbelievable projection is that in Africa, in the near future, there will be 33,000 people becoming Christians every day! How does the Christian Church accommodate growth like that?

How do we, here in America, reach out to people of all cultures, languages, economic status, and race? How do we diversify the Christian church both here in America and abroad? How do we help the growth of the Christian Church in Africa? We have to get past the barrier of people that don't look like us, talk like us, or dress like us. In one local St Louis suburban school district, students speak fourteen different languages! People from all over the World are coming to America looking for a better life for their families or escaping some form of persecution. We don't have to look very far to see mission opportunities - they're right here at home. We have a vital role to play in the spread of the Gospel today in our local communities and abroad.

Ask yourself, do you know, or come in contact with, anyone with a different cultural background or who speaks another language? Do you know of anyone who is new to your community from another country? What can you learn from people of another race, culture, or language? What can they learn from you? What do you share in common with people different from you? Why haven't you met people who are different from you? What's holding you back? What fear or prejudice do you need to overcome to meet people different from you?

Stepping out of our comfort zone as Philip did can be intimidating! But, we must follow Philip's example and step out in faith. First, let's look at what we can do right here in our local community to reach out to people of races, languages or cultures. Begin with prayer and ask the Holy Spirit to open your heart to learn about, interact with, and value people of other cultures, races, languages. Ask the Holy Spirit to guide you to take the time and make the effort to reach out to other people not like you. Look at your neighborhood, church, work, and schools for people that are different from you that you already come into contact with on a daily basis. Then, take the initiative to say hello or introduce yourself. The conversation may end right there and resume at a later time or it may continue with more dialogue. Take it slow, the objective is to learn about each other in a natural and relaxed way. Through building relationships with others and having shared experiences, you can learn about others and come to value and understand them. Long-term friendships begin slowly through honest sharing and caring for each other. Let God bless your time and friendship as it grows the relationship. You will be amazed at how much your life-perspective will change and the ways God uses these friendships to further His kingdom.

Secondly, how do we reach out to people of other races, cultures, and languages that are outside of your community or country with the saving Good News of salvation through Jesus? One way is to ask your pastor about mission opportunities in which your congregation or church denomination participates and how you could be involved with helping them. You could get involved with your congregational mission team and see how your congregation supports mission outreach overseas. Another great way to get involved is to go on a short-term mission trip with your congregation, denomination, or other Christian group.

Above all, we must treat people of other races, cultures, countries, or social or economic status with respect and genuine caring. Discover the ways that you can serve and help them have a better life. Find out what their needs are and how you can work together with them not for them. Serving other people with the love of Jesus is our calling as His disciples. They may look different or worship God differently than you do, but Jesus loves their style as much as He loves your style! And there is so much we can learn from people that look, act, speak, and worship differently.

THE WHAT IF

What if Philip hadn't listened to God's direction to go along the dessert road? What if he hadn't had the courage to go up to the Ethiopian Eunuch because he was a man of a different color or social standing? What would have happened to the development of the Christian church in Africa?

First, it is really hard not to follow a direct order from God. Jonah disobeyed God's calling and look what happened to him! Philip was working west and north in his mission to Samaria, so when he received the vision from the angel, he had to change directions. The Holy Spirit was blessing his preaching and teaching in Samaria and he was just getting started when he received this new mission. He did not know that he was later to resume his mission to the Samaritans. If he did not heed the call to go south, he would have continued his mission to Samaria and God undoubtedly would still have blessed his efforts. But what an opportunity he would have missed! He would have missed out on a golden opportunity to preach the Gospel to people he had probably never dreamed of meeting. The Church would have missed out on seeing an example that the Gospel of Jesus Christ is for everyone.

Also, the Ethiopian Eunuch would have missed an opportunity to know who Isaiah was talking about - Jesus. Here was a man, a God fearer, who wanted a relationship with God but didn't understand all the specifics on how to achieve it. He wanted to draw closer to God but he needed help understanding the words of Isaiah. Without Philip's help, Isaiah and who Isaiah was talking about, would have remained a mystery. The Eunuch would have continued on his journey home with a lot of questions but no answers. It would have just been a regular pilgrimage to Jerusalem and he would have returned home to his regular job, regular friends, and regular life with no significant change because of no Jesus.

Where would the Christian church in Africa be without the contact of Philip and the Ethiopian Eunuch? Eventually the Gospel would have spread to Africa but most likely much later. At the time, Christianity was spreading west and north not south. The Gospel had reached Alexandria but that was one thousand miles away from Ethiopia and in the heart of the civilized world not deep into the center of Africa. When the Islamic hordes swept through Africa years later, without a strong established Christian church, they would have certainly conquered all of Africa for Allah. There might not be any Christian church in Africa today. No billions of Christians now and in the future. Some of the fastest growing countries in the world today would all be Muslim. Christianity would have remained a western, white based European religion. As Christianity is declining in America and Europe, it seems that the future and hope of Christianity lies in Africa. Africa will likely continue to be a powerful force of growth for the Christian church in the century to come.

THE DISCUSSION

1.) During your normal day - at work, shopping, in your neighborhood - how do you recognize opportunities to share your faith? Give an example of a time that you shared your faith (or could have shared your faith) with someone. Why are we so reluctant to share The Good News?

2.) What barriers do you personally need to remove in your heart so you can learn about, and meet, people of other races, cultures, languages? How do you break those barriers down?

3.) How would serving on a local mission project or going on a short-term mission trip (either in America or overseas) impact your faith? How would going on a mission trip impact the faith and needs of the people you would serve? What keeps you from going on a short-term mission trip and how can you resolve it?

4.) Like Philip, you have skills, talents, and life experiences that God can use. Make a list of them. How could you use them to serve your local congregation or your Church denomination?

5.) What resources does your congregation have (time, talents, money, etc.) that could be used to help grow the Christian Church in your community and around the world? Make a list of them. How can you use those resources for mission outreach?

THE ACTION

1.) Visit another Christian Church in your community that has members of another race or culture or economic standing than yours. During your visit, think about the things you can learn from them and the things they can learn from you.

2.) Pray for, and support, the mission outreach of your own congregation and denomination, both locally and internationally.

3.) Reach out to someone of another race, another culture, that you interact with regularly, whether at work or in your neighborhood, and begin developing a relationship with them.

THE PRAYER

Dear Heavenly Father,
Help us to follow the example of Philip. He responded to Your calling as a new generation leader of Your church using the talents and faith in which You had blessed him. His model of character and faith shows us how we too can serve Your church with the talents and faith You have given us. Philip took the risk and the challenge to share the Gospel with people that were different from him. Help us Lord, to step out of our comfort zone and share Your Good News of Jesus with people of every race, every culture, every language so that all the world can praise Your holy name. Amen

CHAPTER 3

THE CONVERSION OF SAUL
"PERSECUTOR REBORN"

ACTS 9

"...SAUL, SAUL, WHY DO YOU PERSECUTE ME?"
ACTS 9:4

The Church was in disarray and the new Christians were being hunted! Christians were scattering all over Palestine and beyond in an attempt to escape persecution. A single man - driven by hate and fanaticism - was trying to imprison, and if necessary kill, any Christians he could find. The stoning of Stephen marked the beginning of the persecution of the early Christian Church. But despite the persecution, it became clear to the Jewish leaders that this new sect, these followers of Jesus of Nazareth, were not going to just fade out and go away. The exact opposite was happening, the sect was growing. The Jewish leaders thought that with Jesus gone, Christianity would die out. They began to look for someone who would lead the effort to wipe out this sect of "The Way" once and for all. Who should come to mind but a young man named Saul who was present at the stoning of Stephen that even urged on the stoning. This young Jewish zealot was just the right guy to lead the charge against the followers of Jesus. He was eager to prove himself as a defender of the Jewish faith - worthy of his training and responsibility.

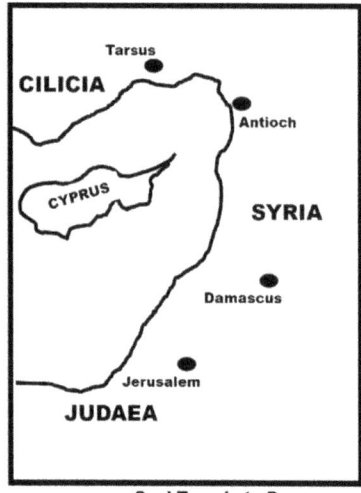

Saul Travels to Damascus

THE EVENT

Saul decided that the best way to get rid of these Christians was to start a reign of terror against them. He began by arresting the leaders to make them an example of what happens to you if you are a Christian. From there he began to hunt down any members who would not renounce their allegiance to Jesus of Nazareth. Saul's spies informed him that the members of "The Way" were leaving Jerusalem and most were traveling north, scattering "like rats leaving a sinking ship". Saul decided that he should follow the members of "The Way" and that the best place to find and arrest them was Damascus. Since Damascus was a big city, the Christians likely believed that they would blend in with the crowds. Saul thought to himself that if he could get the Christians in Damascus, they wouldn't have a chance to head further north to cities like Antioch or west to Tyre and Sidon on the coast where they could escape by ship.

Saul assembled his team of other Pharisees and soldiers and received arrest warrants from the Sanhedrin in Jerusalem to show their support for Saul's mission to Damascus. Saul could hardly sleep the night before he left because he was so excited. He was finally getting the chance to show his love and devotion for the faith of his fathers.

Early the next day, Saul began his crusade. His journey to Damascus along "the Kings High Way" was about 150 miles and would take five or six days. He planned to bring some of his prisoners back to Jerusalem in chains to stand trial in front of the whole city as an example of what happens to those who became a Jesus follower. The fourth day of their journey arrived with the sun blazing down on them as they were surrounded by dust from the horses. They were weary at the end of their day (about four in the afternoon) and looking forward to some rest and dinner. Suddenly, a dazzling light, a light even more blinding than the sun, struck them! It was so bright that they all had to turn and look away because it hurt their eyes just to look at it. Saul was so blinded by the intensity of the light that he dropped the reins to his horse and fell off backwards to the ground.

As he tried to stand up, Saul heard a voice say to him "Saul, Saul, why do you persecute Me?" As Saul tries to look for the source of the voice and suddenly sees the figure of a man covered in radiant light like a thousand suns. "Who are you, Lord?" Saul asked. The figure replied, "I am Jesus whom you are persecuting. Now get up and go into the city and you will be told what you must do."

Then, as suddenly as the light appeared, it was gone! Saul rubbed his closed eyes and when he opened them, he could not see - he was blind! Saul thought that he must have been temporarily blinded by the light because it was so bright. But, when as he tried to make his way to his horse he could feel that there was something covering his eyes. This was no temporarily blindness! He wondered if his face had melted from the light. What kind of man could cause a light that strong? Who was the figure? Shaking violently, Saul allowed his men to help him up. Why were they unaffected? Why was Saul the only one who had been blinded? Saul said to his men

"Help me to my feet. I can't see - I'm blind! You've got to get me out of here. I have a friend in Damascus, Judas. He lives on Straight Street. He'll help me. Get me on my horse, now!"

The group traveled as quickly as they could to Damascus. After locating Judas, the men with Saul left him there and returned to Jerusalem to report to the Jewish authorities about the strange event on the road.

Judas led Saul to a spare room in his house and offered Saul something to eat and drink. But, Saul just shook his head and asked to be left alone. For three days he remained huddled in a corner of the room trying to wrap his head around what had happened. Why him? Why was he blind? Who was he persecuting? What did the man in the light want Saul to do? These were the questions swirling around in his mind. Saul felt like he was going insane! Finally, he cried out, "Yahweh, please help me. I beg you, O Lord my God!"

For three days Saul waited for answers, for healing, for peace! But all he saw was darkness.

Meanwhile, across town lived a man named Ananias, a Jesus follower. He was one of the men Saul had come to Damascus to find and arrest so he could stand trial in Jerusalem and then be sent to prison or even stoned for blasphemy against the Jewish faith. As Ananias was working in his shop one morning, Jesus appeared in front of him and said, "Ananias!" Instantly, Ananias recognized Jesus because Ananias was one of the early disciples of Jesus when he lived in Galilee. "Yes, Lord Jesus," Ananias answered. Jesus told him,

"Go to the house of Judas on Straight Street and ask for a

man from Tarsus named Saul. He is blind and as he has prayed he has seen a vision of a man named Ananias come and place his hands on him to restore his sight."

Ananias replied,

"Lord, I've heard about Saul. He's really a bad guy. In Jerusalem he's arrested and even killed some of us in "The Way!" Now he's come to Damascus with a commission from the chief priests to find us."

But Jesus replied,

"Go! This man Saul is now going to be My apostle and he will preach about Me not only to the Jews but also to the Gentiles. This mission will be difficult and he is going to go through some really tough times. But I have called Saul to serve Me."

Ananias was scared. Could he be walking into a trap? Would he be ambushed and arrested? But Jesus had given him a direct command and no matter how scared he was, Ananias would obey Jesus. Ananias prayed, for courage and then left his shop made his way through the streets of Damascus. He was directed to the house of Judas the tanner. When Judas answered the knock at this door, Ananias announced that he had come to see Saul of Tarsus.

Hearing the name Ananias from his room, Saul shouted for Judas to let Ananias in and silently prayed that this was the Ananias he had been thinking about for three days. Saul prayed that this man would have answers and would help him regain his sight

When Ananias saw Saul, he knew the reason for his command from Jesus to find Saul. He grabbed Saul's arms and said,

"Saul it was Jesus! Jesus of Nazareth - the Messiah - who appeared to you on the road coming to Damascus. He sent me here as one of His disciples to restore your sight and to bless you with the understanding of the Holy Spirit."

Saul immediately felt a burning sensation in his eyes and began to rub them. It felt like skin was rubbing away. He opened his eyes and he could see again! Saul was amazed and shouted,

"Praise God, I'm healed! I'm no longer blind. Thank you, God! Thank you, Ananias! Thank you, Jesus! Ananias, I've been praying for three days about who the man in the light was and who I was persecuting. Now I know! The man in the light was Jesus and I was persecuting His followers. I was blind about who Jesus really is but now I clearly see Him. I understand He is my Lord and Savior. Ananias, please baptize me. I want to change my life and be a disciple of Jesus."

Judas brought over a bowl of water and Ananias poured the water over the bowed head of Saul three times, saying "I baptize you, Saul, in the name of the Father, and in the name of the Son, and in the name of the Holy Spirit." Saul was so excited! His heart was racing and his mind spinning with so many thoughts as he stepped from his old life of darkness into his new life of light in Jesus. Saul invited Ananias to spend the day with him and tell him more about this Jesus of Nazareth, the Messiah, and what it meant to be His disciple. From that point on, Saul became known as Paul and spent his life spreading the Good News of Jesus.

THE PEOPLE

Paul was born in the city of Tarsus in present day Turkey. Tarsus was the Roman capitol of the providence of Cilicia in Asia Minor, a major trading city at a crossroads of Europe and

Asia. Paul was raised in a strict Jewish family of Pharisees, a member of the tribe of Benjamin, named after Saul the first king of Israel and circumcised on the eighth day. Pharisees lived a life of strict observance of the law, keeping their faith and way of life pure and preserving their traditions of their Jewish heritage from generation to generation.

The direct family members of Paul mentioned in the Bible (Acts 23) are his sister and nephew. Paul's nephew reported to the Roman authorities about a plot to kill Paul and this warning saved Paul from assassination. If Paul had only a sister and no brothers, he would have likely felt a strong burden to continue to carry on the family tradition of being a Pharisee. From what is recorded about Paul, it appeared that he gladly accepted this role and responsibility. In fact, he boldly stated that he was a "Hebrew of Hebrews" and zealous for the traditions of his father.

In addition to his family traditions, he was surrounded by a world of Greek customs and culture while growing up in Tarsus. Undoubtedly, Paul had friends that were Greek because he mentioned sports in his later Epistles numerous times. Since the Greeks put great emphasis on sports and physical training, Paul might have participated in sports with his Greek friends. This training may have helped him develop the stamina that he needed later in life as he endured the hardships of travel and persecution. Due to his birth in Tarsus, Paul would have received Roman citizenship because citizens of Tarsus were granted Roman citizenship as a special honor for their service to Rome. Paul used this privilege to his advantage several times in the future.

Paul's education in the Jewish religious practices began at an early age at home where he was tutored by his father. At some point in his childhood, Paul's family moved to Jerusalem and arranged for him to study under the great rabbi Gamaliel. His family must have seen in Paul both a desire to learn their customs and laws and the brains to go with it. Paul says that he was eager above all his classmates to learn the Hebrew traditions and he was top in his class at school. Paul's family had the financial means and the family reputation for Paul to receive such a valued education. After the age of six, a young Jewish boy began his formal education and would spend up to six hours a day learning the stories of Abraham, the prophets, and all the heroes of the Jewish faith in the Old Testament. Part of the school day consisted of learning the Scriptures, usually by memorization. Another important part of his education was language studies. He learned to read and write in the three important languages of his day: Aramaic (the common every day spoken language), Greek (the language of commerce and culture), and Hebrew (the language of the Jewish faith). When Paul turned thirteen, he was received into the local synagogue as an adult so he could further his knowledge of Scripture with readings and debates with fellow synagogue members.

Since being a Pharisee was a religious order, not a paid position, Paul also needed a job. Paul was very proud of his occupation as a tent maker. Likely Paul's father was also a tent maker because it was a tradition to pass on your occupation to your children. Paul mentions several times in his letters that he was proud of the fact that he had a profession that enabled him to make a living and didn't have to rely on someone else's charity.

So why did he hate Christians so vehemently? Paul was a Hellenistic Jew, a Jew born outside of Jerusalem and Palestine, and thus was always trying to prove himself as a good, pure Jew that wasn't polluted by the pagan culture that surrounded his family. He believed that Israel needed a military leader to get rid of the Romans and restore the glory of Israel among all nations. Jesus sure wasn't that guy! Jesus constantly preached peace and taught that God required mercy not sacrifice. Jesus also ate with sinners and even had a tax collector as one of His disciples! Paul thought that Jesus and all Christians were going to destroy all the traditions, customs, and practices of the Jewish faith. Plus, Jesus attacked Paul's fellow Pharisees when He called them a brood of Vipers! Although Paul spent quite a bit of time in Jerusalem, he never mentions that he ever met Jesus personally. However, it would have been very difficult not to have some knowledge of Jesus since Jesus spent so much time in the Temple teaching. Certainly, as a Pharisee, Paul would have heard the talk about Jesus and His disruption to their faith.

The first recorded contact between Paul and Christians was during the stoning of Stephen. Stephen, also a Hellenistic Jew, preached that Jesus was the Messiah at the local synagogue in Jerusalem. When it became apparent through his preaching that Stephen was advocating to change thousands of years of Jewish traditions, he was stoned. Paul stood by holding the coats of the men who were stoning Stephen and watched as this threat to the Jewish faith was eliminated. His participation in the murder of Stephen, and his subsequent persecution of the Church haunted Paul for the rest of his life.

Paul recounted his conversion experience on two occasions: once to a crowd of Jews right after his arrest in Jerusalem and then, a few years later, when he gave his testimony before King Agrippa. He recalls in those two chapters receiving his commission as an Apostle straight from Jesus:

"I am Jesus, whom you are persecuting. Now get up and stand on your feet. I have appeared to you to appoint you as a servant and as a witness of what you have seen and will see of Me. I will rescue you from your own people and from the Gentiles. I am sending you to them to open their eyes and turn them from darkness to light, and from the power of Satan to God, so that they may receive forgiveness of sins and a place among those who are sanctified by faith in Me."

Paul was honored to be called an Apostle, a select group who followed the ministry of Jesus, saw Jesus after His resurrection, and were appointed directly by Jesus to serve Him. Paul's encounter on the road to Damascus with his direct commission from Jesus certainly qualified him for the job! Paul could hardly believe that he, a blasphemer against Jesus, a persecutor of the Church, a violent, disbelieving man was shown such mercy, grace, faith and love from Jesus.

There is not much known about Ananias, except that he was a follower of Jesus and a reluctant hero. In his defense, who wouldn't be scared to face the feared Saul of Tarsus who was actively hunting Christians like Ananias? We are told that he was living in Damascus and he may have fled there from Jerusalem or Palestine when the persecution of the Church began. Jesus chose him to carry out one of the most important and dangerous missions in the history of the early Church, baptizing Saul! Ananias may have wondered why Jesus didn't give this task to a more mature or seasoned disciple, but Jesus was very specific in His instructions to Ananias. Ananias was asked to trust Jesus completely. Through Ananias' obedience, Saul, the persecutor of the Church, was changed to Paul, the protector of the Church.

The news of the conversion of Paul infuriated the Jews and Pharisees. One of their own had betrayed them! Before his conversion, Paul was the driving force to get rid of the Christians. After his conversion Paul began preaching the very thing that he had been fighting against, that Jesus was the Messiah! The hunter then became the hunted as the Pharisees plotted to kill him. But, fellow disciples of Jesus helped Paul escape Damascus and once Paul escaped there would be no stopping him for the next twenty years!

THE EFFECT

The effect of Paul's conversion on the growth of the early Church was profound. His writings and accomplishments take up more books of the New Testament than almost any other subject or person. Paul took his enthusiasm as a new convert to Christianity and began preaching in the local synagogues. However, the Church leaders like Peter and James were skeptical about Paul, and rightfully so when he had been so intent on wiping Christianity out. It would take another fourteen years and a disciple named Barnabas to finally seek out Paul and ask for his help with an important mission for the Church.

Through his missionary journeys, Paul helped turn an obscure local Jewish sect into a world-wide religion of over two billion people today. During his missionary journeys to all areas of the known world, he converted Jews to Christianity and opened the door of faith to all people through his specific mission to bring the Good News of salvation to the Gentiles.

The letters (Epistles) that Paul wrote offered guidance and teaching to specific congregations and helped establish the doctrines of this new religion. Not only were these letters circulated throughout the early Church congregations but they are still used by the Church today. Paul taught on many topics including:
- Jesus is the Messiah and the Son of God
- The wages of sin is death and we are saved by grace
- Our lives are a living sacrifice to God
- We are to respect our civil and Church leaders
- How we are to grow and mature in our faith
- We are to rejoice in all circumstances
- Jesus will return
- How we are to stand strong in our faith and beware of false doctrines and teachers

- The fruits of the Spirit and how to use our Spiritual gifts
- Guidelines for spouses, parents, and children

Another way Paul contribution to the early Church, and ultimately to the Church today, was his emphasis on developing the next generation of Church leaders. Paul devoted at least a portion of each of his letters on how Church leaders were to be chosen, their qualifications, and how to evaluate their performance. There were many preachers that weren't teaching correct doctrines and were harming the early Church as false prophets. Thus, Paul was adamant that the next generation of Church leaders receive proper training and he even directly tutored young men such as Timothy and Titus.

Just as in Paul's day, the Church today is facing intense persecution. More Christians are being persecuted today than at any other time in Church history. It is estimated that over one hundred million Christians around the world are being physically persecuted because of their faith in Jesus Christ. Christians around the world face persecution from totalitarian and Communist governments, criminal organizations, other religious or ethnic groups, terrorist, local tribes or communities, and family members every day. The persecution takes the form of mental harassment, job and housing discrimination, physical abuse, vandalism, and kidnapping, and even death.

As difficult as it is to stand up to physical persecution, it is just as difficult to recognize and fight against the social persecution occurring in the Western world. The accepted morals of our society and the standards of the Bible are in conflict. Mainstream society celebrates legalized abortion, promotes gay rights and passes laws that violate Christian beliefs and practices, even to the extreme of going against the sanctity of gender identity and marriage. Christians are faced with the question of how to stand up for the truths of the Bible in the face being called hate mongers.

How do we, as Christians today, stand up to social and physical persecution as Paul did? A great place to start is by learning about the persecution faced by Christians around the world. Pray for strength and protection for yourself as you stand up to social persecution and for fellow Christians who are enduring social and physical persecution daily. Find out what your congregation and denomination is already doing to help persecuted Christians and pray for guidance on how you are personally called to help. You can also be an advocate by raising awareness about the severity of persecution occurring throughout the world. Go on mission trips so that you can encourage, pray with, and provide support in person to those who are struggling under the oppression of persecution. Another way to offer support for Christians who are being persecuted in the world today is through financial support. There are many organizations that are actively involved in directly helping persecuted Christians. You can also write government leaders to ensure they are aware of the plight of Christians around the world and urge them to provide humanitarian aid and support.

THE WHAT IF

What if Paul's conversion never happened? A lot! To start, half of the New Testament would not have been written! Although God's Church still would have grown, it might look different than it does today. Replacing the greatest early Church evangelist that established so many of the Church's doctrines would have been very difficult. The spread of the Gospel throughout the world would likely have been slower. Yes, there were other missionaries that preached to the Gentiles but none did so with the fervor of Paul. He became the driving force against the Judaizers and taught that you did not have to be a Jew first and a Christian second. He taught that anyone who believed that Jesus Christ was their Lord and Savior was saved by that faith alone and not by following the Old Testament laws, offering sacrifices, or rightly performing the various Jewish ceremonies. Paul's ministry opened the Church to people of all nations.

Other early Church leaders such as John, Matthew, Mark, and Peter were developing the foundational doctrines of the early Church also but Paul had a unique perception and interpretation of the message of the Gospel. The doctrines that were established by Paul and these other great early Church leaders are the same ones that are preached to us each and every Sunday. Along with doctrines, Paul also provided clarity on how to act as Christians. Paul also equipped the next generation of leaders such as Timothy and Titus and it is hard to imagine what the future elders and deacons of the Church would be like if it hadn't been for Paul's instructions.

THE DISCUSSION

1.) How do you respond when God is calling you on a "mission impossible" - asking you to serve the Church outside of your comfort zone? What are the risks involved? How might it affect your faith and the faith of those you serve?

2.) Do you know anyone who (yourself included) was an unbeliever in Jesus and then accepted the Holy Spirit into their heart? Why did they accept the Holy Spirit? How did it change them?

3.) What specific action can you take to help fellow Christians who are being persecuted around the world?

4.) Have you ever faced "social" persecution - been ridiculed, called a hypocrite, been embarrassed by someone because of your principles of faith? How did you respond? How do we as Christians deal with changing social morals that do not match the morals of our faith?

5.) Paul provided instructions (1 Timothy 3 and Titus 1) on specific qualifications for, and skills needed in, Church leaders. Which of these qualifications do you look for in your congregational leaders (all the leaders, not just the pastors)? What qualifications do you have to be a leader in your Church?

THE ACTION

1.) Write down some of your favorite Bible verses from Paul's letters/epistles and then memorize them.

2.) The next time someone criticizes the Christian Church as hypocrites or hate mongers, think of how you would respond to them.

3.) Research what your denomination and Christian organizations (such as The Voice of the Martyrs and Open Doors) is doing to help our fellow Christians facing persecution. Support those organizations.

THE PRAYER

Dear Heavenly Father,
Thank you for the ministry of Paul and the example of how he served Your Church. Help us to serve Your Church to the best of the abilities You have given each of us. When opportunities come our way to witness to others about our faith in You, help us to speak boldly and with confidence our belief in Jesus as our Lord and Savior. Thank you for Paul and others in the early Church who reached out to Gentiles so that we too may know the saving grace of Jesus. Please be with Christians everywhere who are today facing persecution of any form. Heavenly Father, give them strength and courage, remind them of Your love, protect them. And may we today also take action to help our persecuted fellow brothers and sisters in Christ. In Jesus Name, Amen

CHAPTER 4

PETER CONVERTS CORNELIUS
"HEAVEN FORBID - A ROMAN!"

ACTS 10

"THE CIRCUMCISED BELIEVERS WHO HAD COME WITH PETER WERE ASTONISHED THAT THE GIFT OF THE HOLY SPIRIT HAD BEEN POURED OUT EVEN ON THE GENTILES."
ACTS 10: 45

The early Church was at a crossroads. How would they deal with Gentiles wanting to be a part of their new faith? Before He returned to Heaven, Jesus commanded His followers "to make disciples and baptize people of all nations." Did He really mean the Gentiles too? The Jewish people had been set apart as a holy nation, a royal priesthood, in a covenant relationship with God. The Jewish Christians were concerned about what would happen to their traditions and customs if Gentiles were allowed to "join the party." These early Jewish Christians had so many questions and not enough clear answers. But it didn't take long before Peter, the head of the early Church, provided answers.

THE EVENT

Part of Cornelius' daily routine as a Roman Centurion

soldier was coming home during the afternoon to escape from the heat of the day and rest. One day as he was sitting on a bench in the atrium of his home thanking God for his blessings and asking for strength to live each day as a good man that honored the one true living God there suddenly was a man standing in front of him blazing like a bright light! Cornelius was a soldier and had felt courage and fear. In this moment, he felt fear! He knew that this man couldn't be an ordinary guy - not when he was brilliantly lite up like the sun! When the man, an angel of the Lord, spoke directly to Cornelius, "Yes sir" were the only words Cornelius could mumble. The angel then said,

"You are a good man, Cornelius even though you are not a Jew. You honor God by your actions and worship of Him. The Lord has sent me to give you this command: send your aides to a man named Peter who is living with Simon the tanner in Joppa. His house is on the edge of town by the ocean. You can't miss it."

As suddenly as he appeared, the angel disappeared! Cornelius was in shock. He couldn't understand why a messenger of God had come to see him or what the message really meant. Despite his confusion though Cornelius knew he had to send his trusted second in command, Maximus, to Joppa. The journey would be over thirty miles and was potentially dangerous since Romans especially Roman soldiers, weren't welcome in Joppa. Cornelius decided to send others with Maximus and that they shouldn't wear their military uniforms in hopes of blending in with the local population and staying safe.

The next morning Maximus and his men started the journey to Joppa. Meanwhile, in Joppa, Peter returned home about noon after rising early to go to the local synagogue to pray and talk with the members to see what they knew about Jesus of Nazareth. Peter went in search of fresh air on the roof of the house of his friend Simon where he had been staying. Peter was hungry as he'd missed the first meal of the day, so he decided to say his second prayer of the day, the prayer of thanksgiving to God for the food and blessings God provided for him and his family that day. As Peter was praying, his eyes became glassy and his vision blurred. Right before his eyes, he clearly saw a white table cloth floating down from the sky. As the cloth floated closer to him, Peter could see that there were all kinds of animals on the table cloth - just like Noah's ark!

There were animals that he had seen and some he'd never seen. There were even reptiles and all kinds of birds. Suddenly, Peter heard a voice from heaven, "Peter, you're hungry. Go ahead and pick out one of these for your dinner." Peter replied, "But, I can't, I've only eaten Kosher foods all my life. I'd rather starve then eat one of these unclean animals." The voice from heaven spoke again, "It's OK to eat these animals. God made them all. They were all in the Garden of Eden. Don't call a creation of God unclean. Eat!" Peter shook his head no. He couldn't fathom going against all he had been taught. A third time he heard the voice from heaven, "Peter, what is pure to God is not what you eat or the laws that you follow but what's in your heart. Your relationship with God is the most important thing."

The table cloth full of animals slowly disappeared and he heard Simon's wife calling him to come down because there were Romans there to see him. Peter was still puzzling over the vision he had just experienced as he walked to the steps. Then, he felt the Holy Spirit speaking to him:

"Peter, there are three men downstairs looking for you. It might be difficult for you to understand right now but trust Me. I'm asking you to step outside of the comfort zone of your training and traditions. I sent these men specifically to you. They're going to ask you to go with them. Go. Don't hesitate. Go wherever they tell you. Remember, I'm with you, I'm guiding you."

When Peter saw the three men he instantly recognized that they were Roman soldiers. Despite being somewhat nervous about their purpose for looking for him, Peter introduces himself and asks why they are looking for him. Maximus stepped forward and said:

"My name is Maximus. I am the second in command to Cornelius of the Italian Regiment, 1st cohort, Tenth Roman Legion. He is a good commander, a brave leader and he cares about us the men under his command. He has been stationed in Caesarea for ten years and he has adopted the belief in your God and the practices of your faith. He financially supports both the local synagogue and the Jewish community. Yesterday afternoon, as Commander Cornelius was praying to your God, he had a vision. He said it was a messenger from God telling us to come to Joppa to find you at the home of Simon the tanner and then escort you back to Caesarea to meet him. Those are our orders."

Peter replied:

"I'm sure that you had no trouble finding where the tanner's house since you probably could follow the smell for the last five miles. Jewish customs do not allow you as Gentiles to defile us by entering our homes, but Simon, if is it alright, allow these men to rest in your house and get something to eat and drink. Since its already four o'clock in the afternoon, we could not make it to Caesarea before night fall. So, please, rest tonight. We'll leave first thing in the morning. We'll get a good start before it gets too hot."

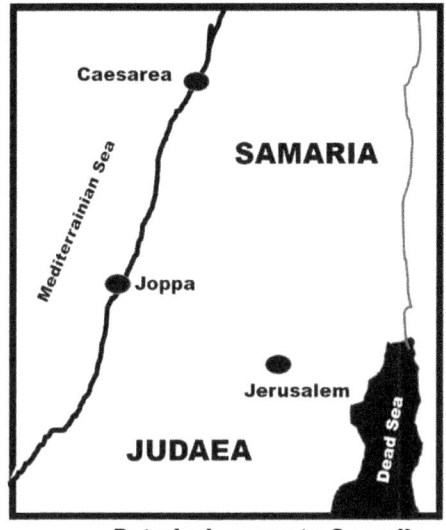

Peter's Journey to Cornelius

Early the next day, Maximus and his men along with Peter and six of his fellow Jewish believers from Joppa, traveled north to Caesarea. When they arrived at the home of Cornelius, a beautiful villa on a hill overlooking the city, a servant led Peter and his friends to the garden in the center of the house where over thirty people, friends and family of Cornelius were standing and sitting. Cornelius rushed to greet Peter and dropped to one knee, bowing his head and kissing the hand of Peter. Peter said to Cornelius, "Get up man! I put my pants on just like you. I'm an ordinary guy - just a former fisherman." Peter then said:

"You may not know this, but it is against our Jewish customs for Jews to associate with you - a Gentile - much less come into your home. This is something I have never done before. But the Holy Spirit told me to do this. Looking at you fine people tells me that I am in the right place. Cornelius, Maximus told me that an angel of the Lord told you to look for me. Please, tell me what happened."

Cornelius explained:

"Three days ago about this time I was sitting right over there on that bench when this man in dazzling white appeared out of nowhere and said, "Cornelius, God knows what a good man you are. Send your men to Joppa to find Peter at the home of Simon the Tanner." So, I sent Maximus to find you right away and here you are. I did a little research about you these past few days and found out that you were a disciple of a man called Jesus of Nazareth whom we executed for sedition. You don't look or act like a man who is involved in treason against Rome. Who was this man Jesus? Is this why you are here? Talk to us. We want to know why this vision that brought you here is so important. Why did God make this happen?"

Peter replied:

"Meeting you after having a vision of my own, I now realize that the Good News is for everyone - both Jews and Gentiles. God doesn't differentiate between Jews and Gentiles so why should we? If you want a relationship with God and the life that goes with it, then you are welcome. This relationship with God is based on the life, the death and the resurrection from the dead of Jesus of Nazareth who we believe is the Son of God Himself. Jesus lived right here in Galilee and Judea. Jesus was baptized with the Holy Spirit by a man named John. Jesus spent three years teaching and preaching and healing people all over this area. He had the power of God in Him and He beat down sin and evil in our world. We were with Him for three years, from the beginning to the end of His mission for our salvation from that sin and evil. Jesus was falsely arrested and crucified. But three days later, God raised Jesus from the dead! Jesus had the ultimate power over sin and death. Not only did the soul of Jesus rise but also His body, the real person we knew because we talked to Him, ate with Him, even lived with Him. Hundreds of people saw Him and are eye witnesses to this fact. You too can know Jesus as your Lord and Savior. Just open your heart to the Holy Spirit and let Him in. It will change your life. Before Jesus left us to go into heaven, where He is now, He commanded us to preach this Good News of salvation to everyone. We thought He meant to every Jew but now I know that this Good News is not just for us Jews but for you Gentiles too."

When Peter was finished talking, a roaring rush of wind blew through the courtyard and through the people listening to Peter. It was the Holy Spirit! Proving that what Peter had said was right! The Holy Spirit had come to the Jews at Pentecost but the Holy Spirit was for all people including Cornelius, his family and friends. The people present were so excited that they couldn't contain themselves. They hugged each other along with Peter and his friends. What a scene!

Peter was in awe and said:

"You have it now just like we do - the Holy Spirit. I am witnessing the outpouring of the Holy Spirit on everyone here. Do you repent of your sins? Do you believe that Jesus is the Christ, the Son of God and that He died and rose again to offer you life and salvation through Him?"

At once everyone gathered there shouted, "Yes!" Peter called for a bowl of water so he could baptize everyone present. Peter stayed with Cornelius for two more days and talked with everyone present about Jesus and the Good News of salvation through Him.

After returning to Jerusalem, Peter was having dinner with some of his friends who were also followers of Jesus. As they were getting ready to eat, one of them named Jacob, looked straight at Peter and said:

"Peter, you are having dinner with us tonight with your fellow sons of Abraham and you act like nothing happened last week in Caesarea. You ate with the unclean, with sinners, vile Romans, uncircumcised Gentiles! Worse yet, you ate with them in their home! What were you thinking? You've never done anything like this before. You are a pious Jew. How could you go against all of the holy laws? What kind of example did you set by doing this?"

Peter jumped up, flushed with anger, and replied:

"I tell you what kind of example I set. It was the example of baptizing people who received Jesus as their Savior. Not only that, but those Gentile were baptized with the Holy Spirit! Before I went to Caesarea, an angel of the Lord showed me in a vision that nothing that God created, whether man or beast, is unclean. Nothing! All of our traditions and laws about what to eat and what not to eat - who to associate with and who not to associate with - they don't matter anymore. It is all about Jesus, our Lord and Savior. Repentance of sin and faith in Jesus is all we need. The Holy Spirit told me to go to Caesarea to a God-fearing man who wanted to know about Jesus. He is a Roman but we were all once lost, just like him no matter if you are a Jew or Gentile, we all begin the same way. We are all in need of Jesus and we can all repent, be baptized, and receive the Holy Spirit. I won't stand in the way of the Gentiles receiving the Good News of Jesus and if I get the chance again to baptize a Gentile, I will do it!"

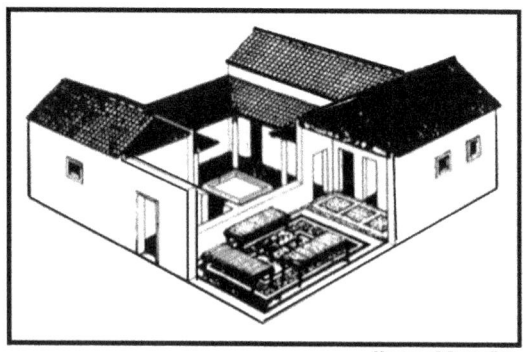

House of Cornelius

THE PEOPLE

In Acts 10 we learn that Cornelius was a Gentile, a centurion, a soldier in the Roman army. He was stationed in the port city of Caesarea, the Roman capitol of Palestine along with his wife and family. He must have served in the location for a quite a while because he and his family had become God-fearers, someone who believed in the one true God – Yahweh – and lived according to some of the practices of the Jewish faith. In his job as an official and representative of Rome, he would have had daily contact with the Jewish people of the city. Seeing how the Jewish people loved and lived out their faith must have greatly impressed Cornelius. As an uncircumcised Gentile, he would not have been permitted to go into the local synagogue but he gave generously to help the poor and support the local synagogue. Over time Cornelius became a respected and trusted friend of the Jewish community even though he was a Roman. We don't know what happened to Cornelius after his encounter with Peter, but he may have been instrumental in helping the early Christian Church in Rome after his commission in Caesarea was completed.

Peter had been a devout Jew all his life. It is easy for us today to think that Peter could simply throw away all of the traditions and customs that had been foundational to who he was from birth. Would you be able to easily change your style of worship or the traditions of your faith that you grew up with, and immediately embrace a new way of living? It was a whole lot harder for those first Jewish Christians than we might initially think. Peter probably struggled all his life with his love for his Jewish heritage and his new found love and faith in Jesus Christ. After his encounter with Cornelius, Peter continued to preach the Gospel of Jesus Christ to both Jews and Gentiles during his missionary travels. Eventually his travels led Peter to Rome and his martyrdom.

THE EFFECT

What is the effect of the conversion of Cornelius on the growth of the early Church? The most dramatic and far reaching effect was that Gentiles could receive Jesus as their Savior, be baptized by the Holy Spirit, and become Christians. Gentiles being Christians hadn't really been considered this before. Jesus was a Jew. Peter, a Jew, was appointed head of the Church. Thus, it was going to be a Jewish Christian Church. Even Peter thought that they would continue their generations old Jewish practices with a new twist. It took a bold direct intervention of God to show Peter that salvation through Jesus Christ was literally for everyone - no exceptions! The Good News of Jesus was for male and female, master and slave, rich and poor, and Jew and Gentile. It was really hard for Jewish Christians to swallow this new concept and many new questions emerged with the realization that Gentiles could become Christians.

Like the conversion of the Ethiopian eunuch, this dramatic event was another example of the Church reaching out to Gentiles - to people of all races and nationalities. How do we, like Peter, reach out to people that do not know Jesus as their Lord and Savior? First, we must acknowledge that apart from Jesus we are sinners with no direction or purpose in life. We need to ask Jesus for forgiveness and commit our lives Him and walk daily with Him and grow in our relationship with Jesus. Then, we need to share the Good News of saving faith in Jesus with family, friends, and everyone we meet when the Holy Spirit opens up opportunities to share. Our job is just to share the story of how we became a Christian and who God is – there's no need for fancy words or long drawn out theological discussions - just simple words from the heart about your own walk with Jesus.

THE WHAT IF

What if the conversion of Cornelius never happened? It certainly would have taken a lot longer for Gentiles to be allowed into the early Church. Peter wasn't the only missionary going to the Gentiles but as head of the Church his seal of approval for the addition of Gentiles to the Church was crucial. He was the catalyst for changing the minds of Jewish Christians about accepting Gentiles as Christians. Without Peter's approval in Gentiles becoming Christians, it would have been very difficult to break down the barrier of faith in Jesus Christ for the Gentiles. Peter said in Acts 11:17: "who was I to think that I could stand in God's way." Peter, the leader of the Church, had to lose his own personal prejudice and tight grip on his Jewish traditions in order to obey God and follow His command that no person was unclean. He learned that everyone can be covered by the saving blood of Jesus and be clean – no matter if they were a Jew and Gentile.

THE DISCUSSION

1.) Who do you know personally that needs Jesus - a family member, friend, neighbor, co-worker? How can you talk with them about Jesus in a natural relaxed way?

2.) How can you recognize people who visit your local congregation? How do you make visitors to your church feel welcomed? How do you invite them back?

3.) How would you approach a friend, co-worker or neighbor to invite them to come to Church with you for the first time? What would you say? What would you do to follow up their first visit to your church?

4.) A lot of people think that the Church is a members only club and that you're not welcomed if you don't look the same as everyone there. What can you do to change that way of thinking? How would you respond to someone who said that to you?

5.) As a disciple of Jesus Christ, what are you doing to continue to grow your faith and your relationship with Jesus as your Lord and Savior?

THE ACTION

1.) Write a short, one sentence, statement about who God is, what sin is, who is Jesus, why you're a Christian, and why you need Jesus.

2.) Be ready for opportunities to share your faith. Remember, your job is just to share your story, the Holy Spirit takes it from there.

3.) Be a friend or mentor to a new Christian or a new member at your local congregation.

THE PRAYER

Dear Heavenly Father,
Help us to be an example of what it means to be Your disciples. Help us to live our lives in service to You and all people. Guide us to opportunities to share our faith in You and to trust the work of the Holy Spirit. Help us to rid our hearts of any thinking or feelings of prejudice and make us open to talking to, and sharing our faith with, everyone - no matter who they are. And help us dear Lord, to reach out to people to make them feel welcomed, to make them feel comfortable, to make them feel part of the body of Christ in our home congregation. In Jesus name, Amen

CHAPTER 5

THE COUNCIL OF JERUSALEM "CIRCUMCISION...NOT!"

ACTS 15

"IT IS MY JUDGMENT, THEREFORE, THAT WE SHOULD NOT MAKE IT DIFFICULT FOR THE GENTILES WHO ARE TURNING TO GOD." ACTS 15:19

The Gentiles were here to stay. They were becoming a part of the Church, but they were so unlike the Jews. They didn't have the same traditions, customs, or laws that the Jews had followed for centuries as God's chosen people. But God chose the Gentiles to also receive the saving grace of Jesus Christ. So how were the Jews and Gentiles to become one united harmonious group of believers in Christ Jesus? As Gentiles began to outnumber Jews as Christians, the leaders of the Christian Church realized that they needed to do something fast or the Church is in real danger of splitting into two factions - one of Jewish Christians and one of Gentile Christians. The leaders recognized that a house divided against itself could not stand and knew that they needed to find a solution to the issues that had the potential to divide the Jewish and Gentile Christians.

As this crisis developed in the Church at Antioch, who was in the very center of the crisis? Paul - of course! If there was a

THE GREATEST FIVE

heated discussion and an exchange of conflicting ideas or teachings, Paul was in the middle of it. When some Jewish Christians came from Jerusalem to the Church in Antioch and started preaching to Gentiles that they had to first accept and comply with the laws of Moses before they could be Christians - boy did that set Paul and his missionary companion Barnabas off! Paul wasn't about to allow these Jewish Christians (Judaizers) to come in and undo the work that he and Barnabas had been doing for over a year converting Gentiles to Christ. Paul and Barnabas appealed to the other members in the Church at Antioch that there was a need to resolve this conflict of teachings. Was the saving grace of Jesus for everyone? Or only for those who first followed the laws of Moses? The members of the Church at Antioch asked Paul and Barnabas to contact the Church leaders in Jerusalem about how to resolve this issue. Paul readily agreed and sent a letter to James (the brother of Jesus) and the leaders of the Church in Jerusalem to request a hearing, the time for a showdown had arrived!

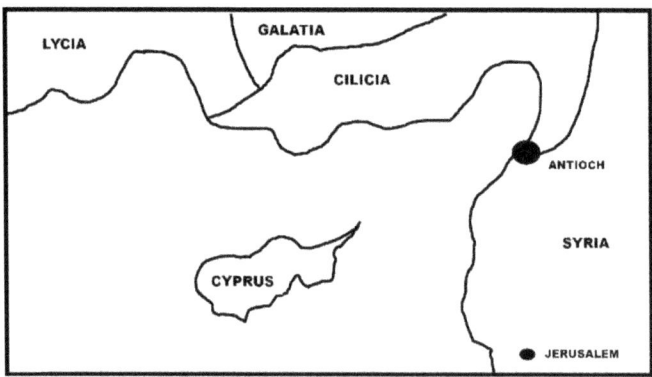

Paul and Barnabas' Journey to the Leaders of the Christian Churches

THE EVENT

A messenger arrived in Antioch from Jerusalem and informed Paul and Barnabas that James and the leaders of the Church would meet with them to discuss their view point about Gentiles becoming Jews, before they become Christians, and whether that meant they must observe the laws of Moses as the Judaizers were promoting.

Paul and Barnabas were thrilled and the next morning they packed their tents and clothes and were on their way. Paul also took along two members of the Church in Antioch, Esau - a Jewish Christian, and Citus - a Gentile Christian.

As Paul and his companions traveled to Jerusalem, they talked with fellow believers in the towns they passed through and all of the fellow believers seemed excited that both Jews and Gentiles were becoming Christians. Maybe it was just a few hotheads that were causing this dissection because most believers were okay with Gentiles being Christians. Although Paul and Barnabas were thrilled that Jewish Christians accepted Gentiles as fellow Christians but they knew that a decision needed to be made because Jews and Gentiles couldn't practice two ways of faith. Paul and Barnabas knew that Christians needed to be united in the way they worshiped and the doctrines of their faith.

Paul and Barnabas finally reached Jerusalem and went to the home of James and to get settled and rest before the big debate with the council of Church leaders. Early the next day, James, Paul, and Barnabas walked across Jerusalem to the home of Joses, a Jewish Christian. His house was large enough to accommodate a rather sizable group of about fifteen men. As Paul and Barnabas entered the meeting room, Paul saw Peter and exclaimed "Peter! It's good to see you. I didn't know that you'd be here. I've been hearing about the great things you're doing among the Jewish Christians." Peter replied "It's good to see you Paul and you too Barnabas. I've been hearing about the great things the two of you are doing in Antioch, especially among the Gentiles. This will certainly be an interesting discussion today. I hope that James can keep this meeting from becoming a brawl!"

When everyone had arrived for the meeting, Paul looked around and realized that he and Barnabas knew James and Peter but he didn't recognize the other eleven men. Paul wondered whether they sympathized with his view of the process for Gentile's to convert or whether they were proponents of being Jewish first. Then, James stood and addressed the council:

"Let us pray: May our Lord and Savior Jesus Christ be with us today, to guide us with His Spirit and to unite us in our mission and ministry for His Church. In the name of Jesus, Amen. Now, welcome to you all. We are here to resolve as Church leaders how we will go forward to unite as one body of believers in Jesus Christ. As leaders, we have been given the responsibility of providing direction to our local Church leaders and members about the doctrines of our faith and how we are to put those doctrines into practice. The question before us today is: Do Gentile Christians first need to accept the laws of Moses before they can be accepted as Christians. Or, can they be admitted into our Church without observing the regulations and traditions of our Jewish heritage? Paul and Barnabas are here from Antioch to present their side of the debate. We also have Ezekiel and his fellow Judaizers who will share their counter view point. Gentlemen, Ezekiel will go first."

Ezekiel stood, adjusted his belt and tunic, and began:

"Fellow Jews - Sons of Abraham - I am a Christian and believe that Jesus is the Messiah. Along with my belief in Jesus, I believe that we all here were raised in our sacred Jewish heritage. Our heritage goes back over two thousand years when God established His covenant with Abraham. This covenant set us apart from all other nations. We are different. We sealed our covenant with Him by accepting God's laws, customs, and teachings. We are God's circumcised people. Jesus was also a

Jew. He was one of us and obeyed the laws of Moses. He came to fulfill the law, not abolish it! Our families, our nation, our very existence would be chaos without our laws to guide us. These are laws that we love. Now we are expected to give up what had defined us and held us together for thousands of years? Can we really just leave them behind as if they never existed just because Gentiles want to be Christians? We've worked hard to follow the laws. Should we really make it so easy for our Gentile friends and tell them that they do not have to put in the same hard work as we do? How do we look our children in the eye and tell them they are no longer a Jew? Is the only thing needed to become a Christian is to believe that Jesus is the Messiah? It can't be that easy! How can we expect people to follow Jesus without following the same laws that He followed? If we are to have unity with the Gentiles, the Gentiles must be circumcised and keep the laws of Moses just as we do!"

As Ezekiel sat down, everyone started screaming at once. James had completely lost control of the meeting. Paul and Barnabas were furious at what they had heard. They couldn't believe that these Judaizers could call themselves Christians and believe such nonsense. Finally, Peter stood and yelled:

"Everyone sit down! Sit down and be quiet NOW! I've heard enough. I've sat here biting my tongue while you, Ezekiel, talk only about the past. The past is gone. We're trying to decide the future! You know that I am a God-fearing Jew and one of the closest disciples of Jesus. You know my credentials. I'm sure you all have heard of my conversion of Cornelius, a Roman. God chose me, Peter, to also preach to the Gentiles. Jesus also chose me to be the rock on which He would build His Church. Today I am that rock. I have witnessed that God gives His Holy Spirit not just to Jews but to Gentiles as well. There's no "us" and "them" anymore. We both have the opportunity for faith in Jesus through the Holy Spirit. How can we burden new believers with the yoke of the law, which we as good Jews couldn't even bear? All of us, whether Jew or Gentile, are saved by grace and faith in our Lord and Savior Jesus Christ!"

The room was totally silent. Peter slowly sat down. Paul and Barnabas were beaming and the Judaizers are squirming in their seats. James turned to Paul and Barnabas and told them it was their turn to present their view. They both rose and Paul spoke:

"Well, I couldn't have said it any better. Barnabas and I came here to Jerusalem to share some of our experiences with our Gentile brothers and sisters in Christ. As you may have heard, Barnabas and I were directly commissioned by Jesus to go to the Gentiles. As contrary as this calling was to my upbringing as a Pharisee, I obeyed the call of Jesus. Barnabas and I spent over a year in Antioch preaching to both Jews and to Gentiles. While Barnabas and I were praying with three others, the Holy Spirit spoke to us and told us to take the Good News to the Gentiles. The congregation in Antioch gave us their blessing and a little money and we started on what became a fourteen-hundred-mile journey. We started out in Seleucia and went on to Cyprus, the home country of Barnabas. From there we sailed to cities in Pisidia, Pamphylia, and Perga. In each city we sat in the town square and talked with all kinds of people and had great success sharing the Good News of Jesus."

"The living God is the one who made our heavens and the earth. He is a spirit, He doesn't live in a temple or stone statue, He is alive, He controls everything that goes on in both heaven and earth. It was God that made us, us men, from one man to all of us today, many nations, many peoples, from the beginning of time until now. He made us so that we would know who He is and what He has done for us. All He asks is for us to believe in Him and to worship Him. He's not in some faraway place but He's here, right here in our hearts and our minds. Our purpose in life is to serve Him and follow His guidelines on how to live our lives. But that's not enough. We let this sin, this evil into our lives. We did a lot of bad things, hating and killing, sexual perversions, saying hurtful things to people, taking advantage of other people, always thinking of ourselves first. Those actions did not bring us closer to God, on the contrary, it drove us away from God. We got so far from God that He punished us with both physical and spiritual death. Because He loves us so much, He decided to help us. He planned a way back, a way to restore the relationship that we had with Him of belief and service to Him and our fellow man. He, God, sent us His Son, His own Son, Jesus of Nazareth, to us. This Jesus lived right with us. But He wasn't like us, He never sinned. Who can do that? We can't, only God can do something like that. Yet Jesus was arrested, tried, crucified on a cross for us, for our sins. He took our punishment for our sins on Him. And then He rose from the dead, the dead! His body came out of the grave. I saw Him. I and others saw Jesus after He rose from the dead. He did it! He conquered evil, and sin, and death. All we need to do is believe that He did it because we are saved by God's grace. There's no way we could save ourselves from sin and death, only Jesus could save us. Just repent of your sins, say 'Lord I'm sorry about the old way of living life, away from you. I want to live life with You. I want Jesus to be my Lord and Savior.' This message of grace of salvation is for everyone, both Jew and Gentile."

"Gentiles in every city we came to, heard us talk about Jesus and some even were baptized. As we baptized these Gentiles, Barnabas and I, like Peter, witnessed the Holy Spirit come on them. After seeing the Holy Spirit coming to the Gentiles, it strengthened my faith that Barnabas and I were called to the right mission. I don't care if I get stoned again as long as Gentiles continue to come to faith in Christ Jesus."

"You're right Peter! This yoke of the law that we, as Jews,

have been carrying for generations is over. Through His death on the cross and His resurrection from the dead, we are saved - by grace alone. All you need to do is repent of your sins, believe that Jesus Christ is your Lord and Savior, be baptized, and receive the Holy Spirit. The work of the Holy Spirit in your life should cause you to change the way you live. Your new life in Jesus will lead you to love and serve God and your fellow man."

Paul slowly sat down. He had finally had the chance to speak about how Jews and Gentiles need to hear about, and believe in, the saving power of Jesus with no strings attached.

Now it was James' turn to speak:

"Thank you, Paul, Peter, and Ezekiel, for your words. I've been sitting here and thinking about what you have all said and I believe that we need to decide today what to do. We need to have a unified mission and ministry. We must put an end to our division and be united. I am reminded of the prophet Amos who prophesied, saying, 'after Israel is destroyed and repents, I will return and rebuild David's fallen tent. Its ruins I will rebuild, and I will restore it, that the rest of mankind may seek the Lord, even all the Gentiles who bear My name.'"

"So, as the head of the new Christian Church, here is my decision: we must not put stumbling blocks in the path of Gentiles coming to Jesus. They won't be required to be circumcised or follow the laws of Moses before they become a Christian. However, we must be adamant that their pagan idol worship practices stop and that they respect the heritage of Jewish Christians. To ensure this, we will ask Gentile Christians not to eat with people who worship an idol or god as part of their dinner practice, be sexually faithful to your spouse, and don't consume blood as it is a symbol of life. These are some basic practices that no Christian should be involved in anyway. We've followed these rules for centuries and they're good guidelines for everyone, whether Jew or Gentile, to follow"

Ezekiel stood and said:

"Speaking for my group, and I think Paul's group would agree, these guidelines are acceptable. We as Jewish Christians can live with these rules and even promote these to Gentiles we meet. What is our next step?"

James wrote an official doctrinal statement that was to be circulated among the established congregations and drafted Barsabbas and Silas to go with Paul and Barnabas to carry the letter on visits to every Church in Antioch, Syria, and Cilicia. The four men were instructed to answer questions about how to interpret the decision of the Church.

The letter said:

"The Apostles and Leaders of the Christian Church in Jerusalem to our fellow Gentile brothers and sisters who believe in Jesus Christ our Lord and Savior. Specifically, to you members of the Christian Churches in Antioch, Syria, and Cilicia and also for the benefit of future Gentile believers in Jesus Christ."

"Grace and peace to you from God the Father and our Lord Jesus Christ. Word came to us in Jerusalem that some members of our Church have been preaching doctrines and practices that we were unaware of and of which we do not approve. These teachings were disturbing to you and may have made you question your faith. So, to clarify the correct doctrines and direction of the Church we are sending this letter along with Paul and Barnabas, whom you know and respect along with two representatives of the Church leaders in Jerusalem, Silas and Barsabbas. You can trust these men! We trust them because they have even risked their lives to preach the Gospel. They will answer any questions that you have about our

Church council decision. We believe that we are saved by the grace of God through Jesus Christ. This is what makes us a child of God and able to receive the Holy Spirit. There are two practices that, if observed, will help you in your walk with Christ. We came up with only two rules because we don't want to burden you with a bunch of regulations to observe to be a Christian. These two rules are both heavily associated with your previous pagan worship practices. One, don't eat any meat that was used in the worship of idols or other gods and usually contains blood and wasn't prepared properly. Secondly, live a life of sexual intimacy with only your spouse. These two practices won't interfere with your fellowship with Jewish Christians and it will remove any sinful practices from your life."

"May the grace of the Lord Jesus Christ and the love of God and the fellowship of the Holy Spirit be with you."

The next day Paul, Barnabas, Silas, and Barsabbas set off on their journey. When they would visit a local Church, Paul and Barnabas would introduce Silas and Barsabbas as official representatives of the Church council in Jerusalem. Silas and Barsabbas would read the Church letter and explain the reasons for this policy and how it applied to each congregation. Silas and Barsabbas both were enthusiastic supporters of the letter and they were very convincing and powerful in their explanation. Both Jewish and Gentile Christians were excited to finally have a clear direction. Their journey took about two months and once their mission was complete, Silas and Barsabbas returned to Jerusalem and Paul and Barnabas stayed in Antioch to plan their next mission trip.

THE PEOPLE

The leadership of James (Acts 21:17-18, Galatians 1:18-19, Galatians 2:9) during the Council of Jerusalem solidified his place as the leader of the Christian Church. James called the council together to address this serious situation, officiated as the head of the council, and made the final decision on Church doctrine. The respect Peter, Paul, and the other leaders in the Church had for James led to the adoption of his decision. James hadn't always been worthy of this respect in the Church. As the younger brother of Jesus, it must have been very hard for James. What an example to follow! Everyone in His family except His mother thought Jesus was crazy and it was a long time before any of them believed that He was the Messiah. While hanging on the cross, Jesus asked John, a non-family member, rather than James to care for His mom. It wasn't until Jesus personally appeared to James (as recorded by Paul in First Corinthians 15) after His resurrection that James believed in Jesus as the Messiah. From then on, James became an Apostle of Jesus and his courage and wisdom led him to be accepted as the leader of the Church. About ten years prior to the Council of Jerusalem, James wrote what is now known as the Book of James, which most likely was widely distributed throughout the early Church. The guidelines he outlined in his letter were instrumental in giving Christians a new standard on how to live their lives for Jesus. There isn't much else written in the New Testament about James, but it seems safe to assume that he remained the leader of the Church in Jerusalem.

Peter's testimony at the Council of Jerusalem helped guide and change the course of the Christian Church. When Peter got up to speak, everyone listened, and he was so well-respected that it was hard to contradict anything he said. As Paul wrote in Galatians 2 that Peter, along with James and John, were the three pillars of the Church's leadership. It couldn't have been easy for Peter to change the religious values that he grew up with, but after witnessing the Holy Spirit filling the Gentiles, there was no way he was going to allow the Church to die by restricting how Gentiles could come to faith in Jesus. There is no further mention of Peter in Acts although we get a glimpse of information that he visited some of the Churches started by Paul in Galatia, Cappadocia, Pontus,

Bithynia, and Asia. Peter was eventually martyred along with other Christians in Rome during the purge of Nero.

After the Council of Jerusalem, Paul was on fire! He had finally gotten the backing of the Church leaders to fulfill his calling to the Gentiles. He had the green light to convert Gentiles without the cumbersome practices of the Jewish faith (especially circumcision!). During his first missionary journey with Barnabas, Paul had seen how eager the Gentiles were to hear and accept the saving grace of Jesus. So why put these Jewish stumbling blocks in the way of their new faith? With the endorsement of the Church leadership, Paul went on his second and third missionary journeys and continued to spread the Good News of salvation in Jesus to all parts of Asia, Macedonia, and Greece. Paul eventually returned to Jerusalem where Jews from Asia who knew of Paul and his work with Gentiles, accused Paul of bringing an uncircumcised man into the temple in Jerusalem. This claim incited a riot and the Roman authorities arrest Paul. Later, after several trials on false charges, Paul was taken to Rome where he continued his ministry and was later martyred for his faith.

Barnabas was also thrilled with the decision of James concerning the Gentiles. After traveling with Paul to Antioch with the official letter of Church policy, he and Paul had a disagreement over whether to take John Mark on their next missionary journey. Barnabas wanted to take John Mark but Paul won't allow it because John Mark had deserted them on their last trip, and there was no room for cowards on missions in Paul's mind. This argument fractured the friendship of Paul and Barnabas and there is no further record of contact between the two men. Barnabas's enthusiasm must have been strained but never dampened, and he continued to preach the Gospel and encourage Christians as long as he lived.

Two new leaders in the early Church emerge from the Council of Jerusalem - Barsabbas and Silas. They traveled with

Paul and Barnabas to distribute and explain the Council's letter. After completing their rounds, Barsabbas and Silas returned to Jerusalem, and, having completed their job so well, they were then referred to as prophets for the way they encouraged and strengthened believers in Jesus Christ. Paul later chose Silas as his missionary partner for his second journey and Peter wrote that he regarded Silas "as a faithful brother."

The Judaizers also walked away with a victory because of the Council's decision. They were released from the bondage of the law by the blood of Jesus and were free to eat, worship, and associate with Gentiles. But the Council had also laid out guidelines that would promote respect between Jewish and Gentile brothers and sisters in Christ with the regulations concerning meat, blood, and sexual practices.

As for the Gentiles, they were now officially welcomed into the Christian Church. Gentiles had heard the saving news of Jesus and wanted to turn from their pagan ways and live for God, but the laws of Moses were totally foreign to them and they certainly didn't want to be circumcised! Now they didn't have to worry about doing anything but accepting Jesus as Lord and Savior before they could be baptized and filled with the Holy Spirit. Not only that, but there was no longer Jewish Christians and Gentile Christians. Everyone was simply Christian with no other distinction.

THE EFFECT

What was the impact of the Council of Jerusalem on the early Church? Wow, what didn't it impact!? All the previous four events in the beginning of the early Church all led up to this climatic moment. The blessing of the Holy Spirit at Pentecost, the conversion of the Ethiopian eunuch, the conversion of Paul, the conversion of the Roman Cornelius - they all led up to this - no more limits to just Jews being

Christians. Faith in Jesus was open to everyone - every tribe and every nation. No more laws to follow, just faith in Jesus as your Lord and Savior and your changed life in obedience to that faith. Paul wrote in First Corinthians that the body of Christ, the Church, is made up of many different parts. No longer were we Jew or Gentile, slave or free, man or woman, but we are all the same in Christ Jesus. In Ephesians 4, Paul echoed this when he wrote "There is one body(the Church) and one Spirit, just as you were (all) called to one hope when you were called; one Lord, one faith, one baptism; one God and Father of all, who is over all and through all and in all."

James and the leaders of the early Church were confident that they made the right decision at the council. There are no limits to who could come to faith in Jesus. However, they also recognized that new believers in Jesus couldn't just go "hog wild" (excuse the term!) and continue to live any way they wanted. As believers in Jesus, they needed to remove any sinful practices from their lives and live a Godly life in Jesus. With this issue resolved, Church leaders could concentrate on developing future Church leaders and further standardize the doctrines and practices of the early Church.

...that the Bible is the inspired Word of God. The Bible is a collection of writings, books, that tells the story of mans relationship with God from the creation of the world until the return of Jesus and how all Scripture points to salvation through Jesus Christ. Man couldn't think up what's in the Bible because its words are from God the Holy Spirit through the faith, the personality, the culture, the experiences of the writers. These are not just made up stories but the Bible is based on actual eyewitnesses, people who personally lived the events and wrote about them. Jesus validates Holy Scripture because He quotes from the Old Testament many times as do the Apostles. The world says that the Bible is a bunch of man made cute stories but we believe that the Bible is 100% accurate. The leaders of the early church from the first writings from around 50AD, began to authenticate and assemble the Books of the Bible that we use today. They made sure that the author was a prophet, apostle or person who had a special relationship with God and had the respect of the people, that man could never have thought up the message of salvation contained in the Bible, that the historical facts in it must be accurate, it was written by an eyewitness or collaborated by eye witnesses and that Scripture validates Scripture, meaning various writers of the Bible mention other writers or other books in the Bible.

…the Holy Trinity, God in three persons, Father, Son, and Holy Spirit. They are coequal, coeternal, same nature, same power ,same actions, same will. God the Father almighty, creator of heaven and earth, created man, watches over us, controls the world, loves us. God, the Son, came to earth to live, to die, to rise for our salvation, to restore the relationship between us and God the Father for eternity. God the Holy Spirit reveals to us the existence of God and the gift of salvation through belief in Jesus Christ as our Lord and Savior, helps and guides God's church on earth, gives us His forgiveness of sins.

…man was created in the image of God and all men fall into sin through Adam and Eve and everyone conceived from them. Man was created with the capacity to love and to make his own choices. God had a perfect plan for man but man decided to challenge that perfect relationship by man deciding what was good and what was evil, what was right and what was wrong not God. By mans fall, mans rebellious action, man rejected God's plan of eternal life and perfect relationship with him. Man chose a way contrary to God's plan, disobeying God, thus brought on sin and death to man. Satan now has his plan which is contrary to God's plan, eternal death and alienation from God for man. Each one of us, all mankind, now has that "original" sin. All humans conceived by a man and woman have it. We are in a state of corruption inherited by us from humans before us as we pass on this inherited sin to future generations.

...we acknowledge the Ten Commandments as one of God's standards on how we live our lives for Him and others. These Ten Commandments are a covenant with God to show Him and others how to have loving and caring relationships between God and all men. We also have a responsibility to teach them to our children from generation to generation.

...the virgin birth of Jesus, Jesus being both God and man, The Incarnation. Jesus was conceived sinless by the Holy Spirit, did not sin in His earthly life, and only as a man would shed His own blood on the cross for our redemption. Only God could live a sinless life and only God could bear the weight of the sins of the world.

...the bodily death and bodily resurrection of Jesus. Jesus as man died on the cross. Jesus as man His physical body rose from the grave.
The death of Jesus on the cross was atonement for our sins. By the death of Jesus, we now have forgiveness, pardoning of our sins. We have redemption through the physical act of Jesus suffering and dying on the cross for us. We have justification, sin is removed from our lives. We have sanctification, we are now restored in our relationship with God.

...Jesus will return again to judge all people for eternity to spend in heaven or hell. Those who have faith and lived their lives for Jesus will enter eternity with God. Those who do not believe in Jesus as Lord and Savior will be condemned to hell along with Satan and all his evil angels.

...we receive the means of grace, forgiveness of sins through the sacrament of Holy Baptism and The Lords Supper. Through baptism we put away the "old Adam", our original sin and renounce sin and Satan in our life, receiving

God's grace and forgiveness of sins. Through The Lords Supper we receive through the bread body, wine blood of Jesus as a means of grace and expression of repentance and forgiveness of sins.

...we are saved by God's grace for us. We are saved from the penalty of death of our sins by the grace of God through the death and resurrection of Jesus Christ not by anything that we can do, it is a gift of God.

...we are called to use our spiritual gifts to serve God, His church, and all people. When every Christian comes to faith in Jesus Christ, he is given a specific power by the Holy Spirit and a responsibility to use that gift.

...we obey the Great Commission. Because of our love for Jesus, we obey His command to share the Good News of salvation through Him with people of all races, cultures, nations.

Another task for the Church leaders would be authenticating the letters that were circulating throughout the Church to distinguish the ones that were just writings from the ones that were inspired by the Holy Spirit and should be accepted as Holy Scripture.

The Council of Jerusalem also impacts us today. By the Council of Jerusalem not making new Gentiles believers conform first to the laws of Moses, it opened the path of faith that we have today. People of every race, color, nationality, culture need the saving Gospel of Jesus. It is our responsibility to follow the Great Commission and go out and reach all people for Jesus. The Church today continues to face issues that divide us within the Christian Church. Issues such as homosexuality, the sanctity of marriage, abortion, stem cell research, and gender identity, just to name a few. We must take our cue from the Council of Jerusalem. Even though we have our differences, we must all acknowledge Jesus Christ, the Son of God, as Lord and Savior who died for our sins and rose again that we too may rise with Him and have eternal life. We pray that we Christians can come together like the Council of Jerusalem and share, discuss, and resolve issues that threaten to divide us.

THE WHAT IF

So, what if the Council of Jerusalem never happened? Like discussed in some of the other chapters, a vital expansion of the Church was to Gentiles. Without a clear directive from the leaders of the Church, the Church might have split into two factions - Jewish Christians and Gentile Christians. Paul and Barnabas were adamant about their direct calling from Jesus to go to the Gentiles. It would have been very hard to stop those guys so it is likely that the Gentile Christian Church would have grown. On the other hand, the growth of the Jewish Christian Church may have been smaller and predominately occurred as Jewish families passed on their faith in Jesus to their children. The question would have remained the same for Jewish Christians through the ages: am I saved by the death and resurrection of Jesus or am I saved because I'm a son of Abraham?

For the Gentile Christians the biggest roadblock after receiving Jesus as their Savior was whether they needed to embrace the teachings of the Old Testament. The Old Testament is where we learn about our relationship with God the creator, humanities fall into sin, the importance of maintaining a relationship with God, and all of the ways the Old Testament points to Jesus as the Messiah, the Son of God. Our faith depends on both the Old and New Testaments! It's hard to understand the life, death, and resurrection of Jesus without understanding of the Old Testament. The law and Old

Testament show us our need of Jesus and help guide us to repentance. If the Church had split in two factions, the Gentile Christians might have lost sight of the need to embrace the Old Testament as part of the Holy Scripture.

The Council also provided an example of how to settle disputes and preserve unity and direction for the Church. Without the Council's direction, disunity and differences in doctrine would have divided the Church before it even got started! Paul wrote extensively in his letters about the need for unity in the Church. The early Church was attacked from all directions. They needed all the strength and clarity of mission to stand against the attacks and survive. Without their example, we wouldn't know how to settle disputes in the Church today. There will always be disputes in the Church because the Church is made up of people who love Jesus, but are also sinners. Sometimes sin gets in the way of fulfilling the mission of the Church of Jesus Christ. We have different ideas, priorities, interpretations of Scripture, and concerns for our faith and Church. Rather than letting these things divide us, we should follow the example set for us by the Council of Jerusalem and dialogue together, share our perspectives, pray for the guidance of the Holy Spirit, study the Holy Scriptures, and then reach a decision, united together in purpose and direction.

THE DISCUSSION

1.) We are the only religion in the world where good works do not save us. There is no way you can earn your own salvation from sin. What does being saved by the grace of God mean to you? How does being saved by God's grace effect the way you live your life each day?

2.) How can the Christian Church as a whole, your denomination in general, and your specific local congregation promote unity among its members? How should you settle disputes and differences in the Christian Church, your denomination, your local congregation?

3.) What are some of the issues and concerns for God's Church today? How do you deal with the morals of society conflicting with the teachings of the Christian Church? How does, or should, the Christian Church deal with these conflicts?

4.) We Christians today have a Jewish heritage of faith. Give an example of what teachings from the Old Testament have special meaning for you? What are some of the same challenges of life and faith that people faced in the Old Testament that we as Christians face today?

5.) How do we stay pure in our doctrines of faith? Where do we draw the line so we don't compromise our beliefs? What happens if we do compromise our doctrines or our core beliefs?

THE ACTION

1.) When you serve God's Church as a member of your congregation, always try to understand the feelings and viewpoints of your fellow members and how you can promote unity with them in your congregation.

2.) Learn about, and study, the doctrines of the Christian Church and the reasons for these beliefs, and then make sure you are practicing them.

3.) Take time to study and learn about people in the Old Testament and their unique relationship with God.

THE PRAYER

Dear Heavenly Father,
We ask for Your Holy Spirit to direct us in our lives and in Your Church. We pray for unity in the Christian Church, unity in our denomination, and unity in our local congregation. Thank you for the leaders of the early Church who set an example of faith, service, and purpose for Your Church. Help us, Heavenly Father, to preserve and protect the teachings of the Church for our generation and the generations of Christians to come. In Jesus name, Amen

CHAPTER 6

FINAL THOUGHTS

Before Jesus accomplished His mission on earth, He left us a great gift, the gift of His Church. During His ministry, Jesus commissioned Peter as the head of His Church: "You are Peter, and on this rock I will build My Church, and the gates of Hades will not overcome it." When the saving work of Jesus was completed, He gave us the Holy Spirit to help us build His Church.

From its very beginning, the early Church had remarkable men and women of faith who embraced the Good news of salvation through Jesus Christ. Through their zeal for their new faith, they proclaimed the Gospel starting from the Great Commission and carrying on through these five events. These five miraculous events of the Holy Spirit shows us today that the challenges, conflicts, and opportunities that those early Christians faced are some of the same challenges, conflicts, and opportunities that we face today as modern Christians.

Every day we experience the power of the Holy Spirit in our lives and in today's Church. Every day we need to share the Gospel with people of every race and culture. Every day more Christians are being persecuted for their faith than ever in history and we need to help them. Every day, no matter if you are a new Christian or have been a Christian all your life, you need to grow in your faith as a disciple of Jesus. Every day we, individually and corporately as the Christian Church, need to stay strong in our beliefs and doctrines.

Hopefully this study of the "The Greatest Five" helped you have a better understanding of the struggles and accomplishments of the early Christian Church and all that we can learn from them

SOURCES

1.) Harper's Bible Dictionary General Editor Pail J. Achtemeier Harper & Row, Publishers
2.) Who's Who and Where's where in the Bible by Stephen M. Miller Barbour Publishers
3.) The Bare Bones Bible Handbook by Jim George Harvest House Publishers
4.) Mysteries of the Bible The Readers Digest Association, Inc.
5.) The Crossway Illustrated Bible Handbook Edited by Tim Dowley. editor Crossway Books
6.) Great People of the Bible and How They Lived The Readers Digest Association, Inc.
7.) The Bare Bones Bible Facts by Jim George Harvest House Publishers
8.) Who's Who in the Bible The Readers Digest Association, Inc.
9.) Illustrated Dictionary of Bible Life and Times The Readers Digest Association, Inc.
10.) The Complete Bible Handbook by John Bowker DK Publishing, Inc.
11.) A B C's of the Bible The Readers Digest Association, Inc.
12.) Jesus and His Times The Readers Digest Association, Inc.
13.) The Message by Eugene H. Peterson
14.) Every Man's Bible New International Version Tyndale House Publish

ABOUT THE AUTHOR

Glenn Sprich and his wife Patti live in St. Louis, Missouri. Both are retired and stay very busy with their four children and nine grandchildren. Patti has served as a parish health nurse and she currently leads a grief share support group. Glenn is active in leading a small group and Sunday morning Bible class. They are members of the Lutheran Church of Webster Gardens in Webster Groves, Missouri.

www.ingramcontent.com/pod-product-compliance
Lightning Source LLC
Chambersburg PA
CBHW060206050426
42446CB00013B/3003